MW01296056

Public Relations Student Playbook

PUBLIC RELATIONS STUDENT PLAYBOOK

Excel in class, at work and in your career

TOM HAGLEY SR.

CONTENTS

INTRODUCTION

Excel In Class And At Work
TOM HAGLEY SR.

The Public Relations Student Playbook provides an unvarnished look at important aspects of the public relations profession. Every chapter cuts to the quick in the style of posts and blogs of useful knowledge on 50 topics based on four decades of practice and award-winning teaching at one of the nation's leading journalism and mass communication universities. The book is not intended to be a textbook, but rather a career companion to students, sharing tips and tactics, assurances and nudges to proceed on pathways forward. The playbook is for students considering public relations as a career, getting started in it and excelling in class and on the job.

October 2019

PART I.

_____

THE PUBLIC RELATIONS PROFESSION

_____

CHAPTER 1.

IS PUBLIC RELATIONS A GOOD CAREER CHOICE?

Is public relations still a good career choice in a society where some people believe liberal arts are out and skills-based, technology-oriented learning is in?

In today's world, it is disconcerting, but not surprising, to see the debate over the value of a liberal arts education versus a technology skills-based education. In the area of public relations, especially, liberal arts and technology skills-based learning should not be held mutually exclusive. By understanding the relationship between liberal arts and technology skills, students with an interest in PR can feel confident in pursuing a liberal arts based degree, and PR firms can feel confident in hiring liberal arts grads.

One thing to understand about liberal arts and technology, like social media, is that to be useful and effective, technology requires human direction. Without it, technology is simply a tool. Social media, with world-gripping interest, are tools until human direction orchestrates the release of their awesome power potential. Value is not in the tools alone, but in their strategic use. Anyone can learn to use Facebook—like learning to use a knife, fork and spoon. But the ability to orchestrate a combination of social media to address a communication challenge strategically requires broad knowledge and that comes largely from the study of liberal arts.

Listing social media on a resume means only that a person has mastered a rudimentary set of skills. What counts is the depth of one's ability to analyze a situation, the cultures involved, mind sets of opposing factions, similar past lessons learned, and other critical data derived from a solid liberal arts foundation in history, psychology, sociology, geography, language, ethics, philosophy, as well as many of the sciences.

In addition to acquiring valuable knowledge, studying liberal arts teaches one how to think, read critically, collect and organize facts, analyze them and form ideas. And you know what else? A strong background in the liberal arts makes one a more interesting person and often produces visionary leaders.

Another thing to understand about liberal arts and technology, like social media, is that when they are combined, they create value. This presents exciting and challenging opportunities for PR pros to serve clients by mapping out strategic deployments of social media to promptly address situations in many areas, such as community, employee, government, customer, investor, corporate and international relations.

Social media today hovers like a cloud of human chatter that sometimes converges on a subject and erupts in thunder and lightening on organizations and individuals. PR pros can use their smarts, educational backgrounds and technical knowledge to orchestrate use of social media, reactively and proactively.

Public relations is still a good career choice, even in a society where some believe liberal arts are losing favor to skills-based technology-oriented learning. Basically:

- PR relies on wisdom from the liberal arts;
- PR students learn to think from the liberal arts;
- PR combines liberal arts and technology to create value;
- PR professionals derive ethics from the liberal arts in delivering and billing services.

By understanding the relationship between liberal arts and skills-based technology, one can feel confident in pursuing a liberal-arts-based degree in public relations.

CHAPTER 2.

THE PROFESSION HAS CHALLENGES

Like other professions, public relations has weaknesses that challenge its members. It is common for a job applicant to be asked about individual weakness. But what about the profession? Can you discuss weaknesses of the profession? You should know the weaknesses and how to meet the challenges

Weakness #1—DEFINITION

There are more than 500 definitions of public relations. You can try to work with that or join others in finding a simpler, clearer definition, like PR is the practice of influencing behavior. Why not? Lawyers practice law. Accountants keep records. If you can't define what you do, you can't measure what you do. If you can't measure what you do, you can't evaluate what you do. If you can't evaluate what you do, no one will pay for what you do.

Weakness #2—PROMISES

Too many people in the profession promise more than they can deliver. The practice is pervasive and could happen with your own staff. You can try to ignore this, but you would be ignoring what is causing an erosion of public trust of the profession and its practitioners. Or you can work with other professionals to heighten the industry's resolve to promise only what it can deliver.

You cannot promise or guarantee results—publicity, turnout, share of market, a winning vote, etc. PR is not a science. Further, there are too many variables over which you have little, if any, control. You can promise that a campaign will be designed to generate publicity, produce a turnout, affect market share or a vote. You can show how the profession draws on bodies of knowledge in the social sciences to create plans to influence behavior through strategic communication. You can promise performance—that every activity in a public relations plan will be professionally executed, and in a timely manner.

Weakness #3—BILLING

Clients of public relations, as well as law and other service firms are not all that happy with the practice of hourly billing. There clearly needs to be a better method of charging for services. You can work under the stress of market resistance to billing by number of hours worked and the value of the person doing the work. Or you can work with others in the profession to explore alternative methods of billing. It's past time for hourly billing to be replaced by a method more acceptable to clients.

Consider, for example, the concept of "pay for performance," not to confuse this with pay for some level of results. Pay for performance can be putting the activities of a PR plan into the form of a critical path or PERT chart, calculating a cost for executing each activity and charging the client for performing all of the activities on the chart in a timely, effective manner. Results derived from a plan could be regarded as a bonus to clients for investing in a plan and the profession.

Weakness #4—LICENSE

Anyone putting flyers under the wipers of cars in a shopping center parking lot can call themselves a PR person. You can brush this aside, but your credentials will wither along with the profession's. Or you can work with PR colleagues to raise the bar for getting into the public relations profession.

Professional status should include some combination of requirements, such as:

- a college degree;
- years and types of professional practice;
- accreditation in public relations (APR) by Public Relations Society of America;
- contributions to the profession as an educator.

Weakness #5—TOOL BOX

You can work out of a toolbox, as too many PR practitioners do. For example, "We can solve your PR challenge with two brochure mailings, some social media, pocket point cards and one news release. Then they throw the tools, like darts to a board, and hope they hit a couple bullseyes to call results. Or you can join other professionals in approaching public relations challenges in a comprehensive manner with credible research, depth of experience and analytical thinking.

Weakness #6—SERVICE

Unfortunately, some public relations firms fall into a cost-driven position. Their overhead cost of operating—for office rent, auto leases, communication, and travel, etc.—puts a priority on paying bills over providing service. The condition for some can be so serious that these firms seek ways to get income by hook or by crook, for example, padding client invoices with excess hours, which is a felony as was showcased with a law firm in the movie, "The Firm."

It is best to set your sights on service. Provide clients with outstanding service, a depth of expertise, high quality resources for graphic arts, photography, research, etc., assertive project management, attention to client direction, flexibility to serve as an extension of a client's staff when requested, and dedication to work until a client's expectations are met.

Weakness #7—EDUCATION

The public relations industry is short of educators—teachers, instructors, professors. Students enter the profession giving little thought to teaching public relations for various reasons. That's OK, but it needs to be understood and remembered that to grow, the profession depends heavily on a dynamic foundation of education and training. The challenge here is to keep in mind the possibility of teaching somewhere in your career future.

If that's a possibility, begin early to collect case materials—photos, illustrations, memos, letters. Maybe keep a detailed journal of experiences to share some day with students. Take photos for later use in class presentations. Save comments from clients. You will be so glad that you took such initiatives in preparation for teaching.

CHAPTER 3.

HISTORIC PRACTICES IMPEDE THE PROFESSION'S GROWTH

Isn't it true that:

- instead of solving problems strategically, many practitioners still throw tools to fix them, like "What you need are some tweets, an e-brochure and two news statements" hoping that some can be called results?

- many practitioners continually resist change as they blindly insist over and over, "That's not the way it's done"?

- some educators teach students what they think clients and organizations want, without knowing for sure what they want and don't want, like hourly billing?

- it's hard to find public relations plans and campaigns of high enough quality to compete in national competition?

- many practitioners use cookie cutter devices, such as communication audits, news releases, and newsletters, rather than constructive, analytical thinking?

- clients still feel that practitioners tell more than they listen, that is, when a client asks for a Mac and gets Nuggets?

- many practitioners cannot explain the difference between a goal, objective and strategy?

- the profession still struggles to define itself and its effectiveness in ways that are readily seen of great value not just to itself, but to clients as well?

If these comments are professionally disturbing to you there's hope; if they aren't, they should be.

CHAPTER 4.

ITS MARKET VALUE DEPENDS ON HOW PUBLIC RELATIONS IS DEFINED

Test the market value of the definition of public relations. There are more than 500 in use today. Would an employer pay, for example, a salary of $100,000 a year for you to perform what you define as public relations? Following is how I arrived at a definition that has a high market value.

I like to challenge people to define public relations in two words. Other professions define themselves in two words—doctors practice medicine, lawyers practice law, accountants keep records. People in these disciplines define their work in two words, issue invoices and get paid accordingly for their expertise. Not everyone in PR can do the same because many people—yes, many people— in public relations cannot define what they do. If you can't define what you do, you can't measure what you do. If you can't measure what you do, you can't evaluate what you do. If you can't evaluate what you do, no one will pay for what you do.

To arrive at a two-word definition of public relations, I looked back over the years, made a list of untold numbers of projects and programs I had completed and summarized them as follows: I persuaded people to support, to vote, to consider, to champion, to follow, to read, to buy, to trust, to invest, to listen, to join, to leave alone, to contribute, to believe, to work, to authorize, to accept, to welcome, to compromise, to accommodate, to cooperate, to wait, to decide and the list went on and on and on. The common denominator, the two-word definition, became perfectly clear. That is, in public relations, we "influence behavior." Whose behavior do we influence? The answer for a public corporation, private company and for a not-for-profit organization is the same. We influence the behavior of anyone who has or could have an effect—positive or negative— on the organization's ultimate performance. That would include, as examples, employees, suppliers, customers, shareholders, labor unions, voters, government regulators, special interest groups and many more.

Is that ethical? Of course it's ethical. The ethical principles applied to PR are no different than those applied to any other profession. Is it ethical to persuade someone to replace a heart, a tooth, a roof or a brake cylinder? Certainly it's ethical if one does, in fact, need to be replaced.

How do we influence behavior? We influence behavior through strategic communication. And therein lies the "magic of the profession" that few PR practitioners possess and for which fewer still get proper recognition. True expertise in strategic communication is hard to find. That's why I call it the "magic of the profession." Strategic communication requires knowledge, skills and problem-solving experience in the dynamics of persuasion, human interaction and communication design. In public relations, we influence behavior through strategic communication. How do we evaluate our effectiveness? The answer, simply: Did we influence behavior or not? Trust me; employers and clients like measurable public relations. So what is public relations? It is influencing behavior through strategic communication.

CHAPTER 5.

WHAT IS JARGON DOING TO THE PROFESSION?

Why do PR and marketing professionals make up and use jargon that only they can understand? That just creates a bigger chasm in understanding between clients and these two big "communication" industries. It also confuses entry professionals who already question their ability to work with business people with whom they feel a disconnect.

Getting a more educated understanding of business is fine, but aside from signing up for MBA courses, there is something you can do to close the gap between communication and business professionals. That is getting rid of meaningless public relations and marketing jargon.

To illustrate the damage jargon is doing, read the following mock pitch to business written entirely with jargon from an article titled, "20 Insightful PR and marketing predictions for 2018," produced with contributions from PR/marketing "professionals" and published in the Sword and the Script newsletter. Hopefully this will heighten your interest in avoiding the use of meaningless jargon. Here is the mock pitch:

Mr. Business Client,

Public relations/marketing predictions for 2018 are at **an intersection of analysis and aspiration...** As you know, my firm practices **pay for play**. We use **AI tools and competencies to deal with convenience and friction**, mostly to **minimize friction**. Our specialty is **influencer relations**, with an emphasis on **micro-influencers**, **real influencers** and **paid influencers** to develop plans for the **fragmentation of influence**. Your focus is **customer-centric** and **100% transactional**. We completely understand your **content marketing niche** and the increased need for more **content-driven conversations** and to avoid any more **hyper-targeted vapid rehashes**. We will show you how to **extract value from your subscribed audiences** using **multi-touch campaigns** rather than **the mar-tech stuff**. There's a **CRM system** we would like you to see that **drives engagement**. We also found a way to **execute a strategy of tactics to deliver opportunities that drive alignment and growth**. Unfortunately, in this **data-driven arms race**, there has been **a laxity in removing content**. But we can cut through the **digital noise**. That opens more **opportunities to amplify clients' content**. You must pay attentio**n to A/B testing, personalized web experience and algorithmic signals**. There has been **an explosion in tools that mash-up and create dashboards** plus **new tools that chew on data to help provide action guidance** on what to do next. We are tracing a pathway to **purchase actions** and to using **physical world touches**. We never follow **bureaucratic marketing practices**. We are experts in **re-engineering marketing organizations** to give clients what they want in the years ahead. These are our insightful PR and marketing predictions for the coming year.

CHAPTER 6.

WHAT'S IT LIKE TO 'SELL' PUBLIC RELATIONS SERVICES?

Prospective Client

CLIENT: Let's cut to the chase. Why should I spend money on public relations?
ACCT EXEC: Public relations gives you the ability to influence human behavior.

CLIENT: What does that mean?
ACCT EXEC: It means that PR can help you motivate people to support, to vote, to consider, to champion, to follow, to read, to buy, to trust, to invest, to listen, to join,

to leave alone, to contribute, to believe, to work, to authorize, to accept, to welcome, to compromise, to accommodate, to cooperate, to wait, to decide and the list goes on and on as you can imagine.

CLIENT: How does it do that?
ACCT EXEC: Public relations influences the behavior of people through persuasion.

CLIENT: So PR uses devious means to manipulate people?
ACCT EXEC: There are two sides to everything people do—good and bad. PR influences behavior honestly and ethically through strategic communication.

CLIENT: How does this work?
ACCT EXEC: PR plans, one can say, mirror the process of persuasion. PR sets objectives to accomplish a goal. It taps into the field of persuasion to design actions to influence an individual, group, or organization toward achieving the goal. A number of objectives, each for a particular target audience, might be required to achieve a goal.

CLIENT: Be more specific.
ACCT EXEC: Specifically, here's an example of persuasion: Let's say a person, like a stock broker, takes an action (recommends a stock selection), to a target (potential investor), designed to cause a particular behavior (to buy the recommended stock). An objective in a public relations plan is similar to the persuasion process, in that it has three parts: 1) an action to be taken; 2) a target, or receiver of the action; and 3) a behavior desired of the target as a result of the action taken.

CLIENT: Give me an example.
ACCT EXEC:

Action—inform about skyrocketing cost of medical insurance

Target—employees

Desired Behavior—willingness to share the company's cost of medical insurance

Objective—To inform employees of the company's skyrocketing cost of medical insurance so they become willing to share part of the increased cost.

CLIENT: How do you assess results?
ACCT EXEC: You can assess results on the basis of performance (Was the public relations objective carried out completely, accurately, on schedule and budget?) and effectiveness (What was the outcome: a. attempts to influence failed; b. influence attempts got attention; c. influence attempts achieved the desired behavior?)

CLIENT: Are all PR people trained in persuasion?
ACCT EXEC: That's a good question to ask when you interview job candidates and PR firms. Many PR people have a solid background in persuasion derived from a broad liberal arts foundation in history, psychology, sociology, geography, language, ethics, philosophy, as well as many of the sciences. In acquiring this valuable knowledge they have learned to think and read critically, collect and organize facts, analyze them and form ideas. They have the ability to analyze a situation, the cultures involved, mindsets of opposing factions, similar past

lessons learned. They also draw upon the profession's body of knowledge of actual experiences.

Public relations is the practice of influencing behavior through strategic communication and is a profession that holds itself accountable for cost, completeness, effectiveness and measurability.

CHAPTER 7.

WHAT'S YOUR PREFERENCE: PRACTICING PR OR TEACHING PR?

Some want to move into business. Some want to move into education. Here are some deliberately provocative contrasts in career areas that might stimulate some conversation.

- In business, you shape your agenda daily by whatever you decide is most important, or by what is unexpectedly demanding. In education, you follow a classroom agenda predetermined by a syllabus you created in advance to follow for a period of time.

- In business, an immediate supervisor with a focus on your job description judges your performance. In education, students with a focus on themselves judge your performance.

- In business, in addition to doing a good job, you have to be seen, heard and championed frequently to keep it and progress. In education, you focus on tenure.

- In business, you apply different skills to serve others in a variety of disciplines, such as marketing, finance, human resources, engineering, etc. In education, you apply teaching skills to serve students.

- In business, performance is scrutinized daily on specific observable criteria and feedback from internal and external "clients." In education, performance is self-assessed annually in terms of progress made in teaching, research, service, student advising and further career development.

- In business, solving problems, getting results, dealing with the unexpected and winning the respect of others is a mental preoccupation that is in relentless competition with other aspects of one's life. In education, good planning and time management in a predictable environment facilitate a balanced life style.

- In business, your good efforts are recognized and rewarded from the top down. In education, recognition is applied for from the bottom up and is very slow in materializing.

- In business, you get one shot at succeeding with projects. In education you get multiple opportunities in everything to improve and succeed.

- In business, career risks rise exponentially with increases in high-profile responsibilities. In education, career risk is minimal.

- In business, salaries are set to a range of skills and responsibilities. In education, salaries are subject to fixed budgets.

- In business, loyalty is rewarded, in part, by employment incentives. In education, loyalty is not expected.

- In business, mistakes, while not life-threatening, have consequences. In education, mistakes are welcomed as learning experiences.

- In business, stress to succeed is unhealthy. In education, stress to succeed is a positive motivator.

- In business, pay is high. In education, pay is low.

CHAPTER 8.

SUCCESS IN THE PROFESSION REQUIRES A STRATEGY

You can achieve your career goals faster and, more efficiently, when you have a strategy. No matter where your career begins—in education, business, the arts, sports, government, public relations—you will accelerate your professional growth and development when you follow a success strategy. To get you started in developing a strategy, I am going to ask you to give up three commonly held notions, replace them with real actions, and consider five basic tactics to put you on a road to success in your career.

You might find what I suggest to be uncomfortable. But

rest assured, I'm not urging you to change who you are. Rather, I am urging you to make the most of who you are to achieve what you want to achieve. Let's begin by confronting three false notions.

#1 Success happens.

First, we have to acknowledge that success doesn't just happen. You cannot count on getting ahead solely on the merits of your work. You cannot count on getting ahead as a workaholic. You cannot count on getting ahead by hoping you will be promoted as the right person at the right time for the job. You must break away from the notion that success happens and pursue an enlightened view of what it really takes to progress in a career using tactics soon to be described.

#2 My career is in good hands.

Next, we have to acknowledge that putting your career in someone else's hands is like believing in Santa Claus—like believing a superior who says, "Stick with us, we have great plans for you." You must take charge of your own career. Put yourself behind the wheel of your career, making timely decisions to go here, there and anywhere that seems interesting and exciting. Time is wasted, waiting for someone to promote you. You must set your own timeline as to where you want to be in your career and when, and use the tactics about to be described to get where you think you should be.

#3 Opportunities will come along.

Next, we have to acknowledge that hoping for opportunities is an excuse for inaction. You must stand out from the competition—you need to compete. Not everyone likes to compete with others, but you must distinguish yourself from the competition in the eyes of those who have the authority to provide advancement opportunities. Leave this notion behind and use the tactics about to be described.

So, in developing a success strategy, you need to be realistic in your pursuit of a career, take charge of making career decisions, and distinguish yourself from the competition.

Following are five basic tactics for developing a success strategy. Included with each one is a personal assessment scale for you to mark today, and again, one month later to evaluate your progress. You should customize and add to these basics to make this strategy your own.

KNOW YOUR ENVIRONMENT

is one tactic for developing a success strategy. The natural tendency in starting a new job is to focus sharply on doing what you're expected to do. But in the process, it's important to look around. View the organization from top to bottom. Learn the politics. Know who has power—who makes the big decisions. Is there a group of individuals that seems to run the organization? If so, who are its members? Think about how you can get to know each one. In your job you likely will have reason to call on these individuals. Assist them in writing messages, letters, speeches, memos, etc. Learn to think like a senior manager.

A word about gender… As you assess the organization, if you sense that managers don't believe in and support a positive, flexible organization with open communication that fosters a positive environment equally for women, pack your bags and look for a better employer. Trying to break through a glass ceiling is stressful and a waste of time. Find a place in which you can compete fairly to succeed in pay and position. .

Personal Assessment

How well do you know the work environment today? (1 to 5 hi)

What must you do to attain a high score?

How well do you know the work environment one month later? (1 to 5 hi)

BE SEEN

is another tactic for developing a success strategy. People have expectations of public relations people. Be aware of the expectations of others and try to meet them. Your presence will be expected at certain functions. Make room in your schedule to make appropriate appearances. Make yourself and your accomplishments visible to others. You can come up with subtle ways to blow your own horn or have others do it for you. Participate in high-profile projects and activities. Volunteer to make presentations and to give reports. Don't let yourself fade into the background. Don't walk out of a meeting wishing you had spoken up and expressed an opinion. Take the initiative to be seen as you want to be seen. If you want to be seen as a counselor rather than a technician, don't carry a pencil behind an ear, a camera around your neck, a clipboard in your hand.

Personal Assessment

How well are you seen (known) in the work environment today? (1 to 5 hi)

What must you do to attain a higher score?

How well are you seen (known) in the work environment one month later? (1 to 5 hi)

BE HEARD

is another tactic for developing a success strategy. Being a thinker and doer is not enough. You need to talk to excite and inspire people about what you do and what you believe. You need to let people know what you're doing and why it's important to the organization. Others will harbor an ignorant view until you tell them what you do. Don't worry about using 20 percent of a day educating others on your work. The investment will show great returns.

Anticipate opportunities to express an opinion. Don't wait around. Use every minute available to plan in advance good comments to make. Research items that are likely to be discussed. The quick acquisition of knowledge is a powerful tool. Write down your thoughts and possible points you want to make. Practice delivering aloud key statements. Do not believe that what you want to say will come to you just when you have the opportunity to be heard. Only birds can wing it.

Assert yourself to make your opinions known. Make your comments brief and to the point. Never qualify your ideas and suggestions. For example, never begin a suggestion with, "This is just a thought…" or "You know more about this than I…" or "I'm not sure if this would work…" There's nothing wrong with saying, "One thing we could consider…" or "There's one thing we haven't talked about…" Plant the seed and leave it there on the conference table to grow. Give others a chance to help you cultivate it. Before you know it, someone will say, for example, "Jerry had a good idea at our meeting last week." When you do speak out, it's important to sound confident.

If a person seems sure of himself or herself, a senior manager will be more inclined to pay attention. Executives make decisions quickly with limited information. They judge the validity of the information based on their perception of the source.

There's a certain amount of risk in taking the initiative to be seen and heard. But risk is inherent in the profession. As you assume greater responsibilities, you take on bigger, more visible projects and you become directly associated with their success. But be selective. If it's not in the public interest don't do it. If you don't have the resources to do it right, don't do it. The results of your performance are there for everyone to judge. Don't back away from the spotlight. Maintain the highest possible standards of work and enjoy the recognition. Speak to excite and inspire others. Plan your initiatives. Speak with confidance. Strive for perfection. Enjoy the spotlight when it shines on you.

Personal Assessment

How well are you heard in the work environment today? (1 to 5 hi)

What must you do to attain a higher score?

How well are you heard in the work environment one month later? (1 to 5 hi)

BE WELL SPONSORED

is another tactic for developing a success strategy. Being well sponsored means having a broad base of people who know and appreciate what you do and the value you add to the organization. Having such champions is essential at critical junctures in an organization, such as a changing of the guard (changes of top management), downsizing, restructuring, merging or acquiring. You want colleagues to say, "We need Sally, or George," for example. It's important to be accepted as a highly valued member of the organization.

Being well sponsored means building relationships. You have a mind to decide what you want to be to others. Whatever that is, be consistent and predictable. Listen attentively when people talk to you. Take a genuine interest in co-workers and clients; give them 100 percent of your presence. That means being polite enough to keep your cell phone out of sight. Saying, "I have to take this," is rude behavior and tells others that they are not as important as your callers. It tells clients they should find another consultant or agency. Look for ways you can help others in their work (e.g. drafting a message, letter, memo, etc.). Deliver what you promise. No excuses. People pretend to forgive, but they never forget how you let them down. Learn the role of a ghostwriter. It is, in large part, to help others develop something that will capture the interest of people, which will shower them with praise and recognition. So put your ego away. Write the song, so to speak, and let the performer sing it and receive the applause.

Being well sponsored means having a network of friends and colleagues you trust and who respect you— people who support and encourage each other. They can be instrumental in helping you find your next advancement opportunity or next employer. Think about the image you want to project. You will want to get to know people. Help them get to know you and feel comfortable with you. As you develop relationships, think about finding mentors. Consider getting yourself a cheerleader. Find someone who truly believes in you. Someone who will convince you to take reasonable chances and do what you really can do and know you must do. Mentors are invaluable. They can:

- accelerate your professional development—tell you what skills and education are important for advancement;
- have others take notice of you and your work;
- be sounding boards for ideas and plans;
- provide political insights on how the organization operates;
- identify roadblocks and blind alleys and point you

in the right direction;

- be your advocate, get you appointed to important committees;
- advise which jobs to take and which to avoid;
- can facilitate your acceptance into inner circles;
- can help you meet the right people.

(A note about gender... There is understandable concern of women that seeking mentoring might be misconstrued as seeking a date. Keep in mind that mentoring relationships can be formal or informal. There's no need to ask, "Will you be my mentor?" You can accomplish a mentoring relationship by asking for help on a project and expressing your gratitude by saying, "Your advice was a great help. Could I call on your help again, if I need advice?") Being well sponsored means developing a broad base of champions, building relationships, developing a network, and acquiring mentors.)

Personal Assessment

How well sponsored are you in the work environment today? (1 to 5 hi)

What must you do to attain a higher score?

How well sponsored are you in the work environment one month later? (1 to 5 hi)

CHALLENGE YOURSELF

is another tactic to use in developing a good success strategy. It's common to feel that you can't do something, or to be afraid of failing, to feel you are too young or inexperienced, or that you're not skilled enough. Believe me, there isn't much a person can't do if you challenge yourself.

Start with the easy part. Think about how you interact with people. Do you speak to others eye to eye? Do you smile often and naturally? Do you appear to be your own person? In other words, do you give the impression that you think for yourself? Are you respectful of other generations and their feelings? People born in the '40s and '50s differ from younger people in what they expect in professional behavior, attitude, social graces, treatment of those with considerable experience and position. Yes, the world is changing, but PR agencies have lost clients over the matter of respect for other generations.

Sometimes taking on challenges feels like you just can't take the first big step. Try this. Write down what you need to do. If you are planning an event, for example, close your eyes and walk through the experience from beginning to end in every detail as a guest. Know that attention to detail is what makes events memorable. Identify and assess potential obstacles. Plan strategies to pursue and overcome the obstacles. Write down reasons why you are reluctant to pursue your plan. Address those reasons head on. Good planning helps assure success. Also know that while high-visibility errors can be painful, they are not life-threatening. Pursuing tactics in a success strategy isn't the easiest thing in the world to do. It might even make you feel faint or sick to your stomach. Those are natural feelings. Everyone has them to one extent or another. There's no need to change who you are. Be yourself.

Establish principles for yourself. For example, always take the high road—practice statesmanship. In other words, seek solutions to problems that are in everyone's best interest, or in the public's best interest. Influence people on the merits of the argument. Address issues, never attack their advocates whose support you might need in the future. When someone treats you unfairly, rather than seek justice, let justice catch up with the individual. It will. If you start to see obstacles, review the goal. Re-orient yourself. Take a break, relax and let the creative juices flow on their own. Have a mocha. When the right idea pops to mind, take the step and it will take you to the next level of accomplishment.

Challenging yourself with these tactics isn't easy and it doesn't mean you have to enjoy the experience. The joy is in proving that you can do it. The joy is in having done it and in planning your next move.

Personal Assessment

How well are you challenging yourself in the work environment today? (1 to 5 hi)

What must you do to attain a higher score?

How well are you challenging yourself in the work environment one month later? (1 to 5 hi)

PART II.

GETTING STARTED IN THE PUBLIC RELATIONS PROFESSION

CHAPTER 9.

ARE YOU UP TO THE CHALLENGE AS AN ENTRY PROFESSIONAL?

There are two ways to enter the public relations profession. One is to walk in the front door and go to work. Another is to prepare in advance for walking into a work environment that requires much more than just going to work.

It used to be that PR professionals were looked to for error-free punctuation, spelling, grammar and journalistic style. Today public relations practice has greatly increased responsibilities relative to honesty, integrity, trust and civility.

Professionals must deal with people who have no compunction about saying whatever they want, whenever they want, however they want. They must deal with today's unabashed use of underhanded communication tactics that have fostered a nationwide climate of blameworthy behavior.

Such underhanded communication tactics include:

- Tell a falsehood repeatedly and it becomes believed.
- Win support by saying whatever people want to hear.
- Respond to what you don't like by calling it fake.
- Confront criticism by attacking the credibility of the source.
- Divert attention from one issue by "making up" a bigger one.
- Face off adversaries with derogatory name calling.
- Show superiority by denigrating character.
- Use false leverage to project authority.

- Bolster image by falsely claiming success for anything.
- Show strength by "throwing people under the bus," w/o compassion, empathy or regrets.
- Use unsubstantiated claims to declare success.
- Show superiority by belittling ethnicity.
- Dismiss intelligent thinking by ignoring it.

Evidence of such tactics is showing up in substantial segments of society, especially by groups of people outwardly set on getting their own way at any cost. For professional communicators, the effects of underhanded tactics can be expected to surface at any time, to any degree, in any target audience. It is a factor that must be considered in developing public relations programs.

In advance of walking into a new job environment, entry professionals should equip themselves intellectually with a resolve to know and stand up for the ethics of the profession. Not only must they be moral agents discerning right practices from wrong, but learning how business operates and is challenged inside and out by the social behaviors of society. An entry-level position should be seen as a privileged look inside a profession, an opportunity to learn the language of professionals and explain what they do and how they do it, and the first of many steps in working critically and creatively toward a successful, life-long career.

CHAPTER 10.

GET MORE OUT OF PR CLASSES

Class time is your time. You're paying for it. Why rely solely on a professor to make the most of it for you? Consider some tactics you could pursue to make your classes more interesting and worthwhile.

- Come to class the way you would like an employer to see you come to work. Show off some personal character traits that you would like to see reflected later in a letter of recommendation from your professor.

- Practice greeting your classmates as you plan to greet colleagues at your first job. Think about how you would show others that you're a team player.

- Be up on current news events every day and ready to relate them to class discussions to get into the habit of scanning news for an employer or client.

- Give some serious thought to the electronic devices you use habitually. Use the class period to time keeping them turned off and out of sight. This drill will prepare you for when a client, paying you more than $100 a hour, demands 100 percent of your presence.

- Treat homework, done electronically or on paper, as a superior product, a work of art, to prepare for when you will be invoicing a client $5,000 for a speech, or $2,000 for a news release. Use your keyboard the way an artist uses a palette to express your thoughts creatively, and feel proud to present your work.

- Take on the challenge of developing a genuine working relationship with your instructor/professor as you will have to do with future job supervisors.

- When your class has a guest speaker, practice making first impressions. Introduce yourself and hand the guest one of your business cards with your contact information and title as:

MARIE SMITH

Outstanding Job Candidate

(Name of university)

000 xxx-xxxx   (E-mail address)

CHAPTER 11.

GET WHAT YOU WANT FROM INTERNSHIPS

Some internships fit students right in with a team to help with a project. Some provide opportunities to back up staff with research, writing and editing. Some provide short assignments, routine chores and phone calling with empty gaps of time between them. You need to know how to get what you want from internships.

How you enter an internship determines what you will

get out of one. If you enter acting like an indentured servant expecting close supervision and instruction, you most likely will leave feeling relieved that your servitude is finally over. However, if you enter with a plan and execute it well, you are likely to leave feeling like a runner, now in even better shape to meet the next challenge.

You need to decide that you are going to make the internship about learning, winning friends and having fun. No one is going to do all of that for you. You have to take personal initiatives to turn your space into a field of positive energy that others can feel and enjoy with you.

You need to fill empty gaps in work by taking an interest in what others are doing and suggest ways to help. Ask to sit in on meetings, discussions, practice presentations. Your supervisor will love getting some relief from continually trying to find things for you to do.

You need to offer creative ideas. Don't claim you're not a creative person, that you're missing certain character traits. To me, creativity is thinking up ideas that others haven't thought of. So offer your ideas and don't apologize for them, with "This might not be very good, but…" Plant your ideas, like seeds, and let them grow in other heads.

Winning an internship is admirable! It opens the door for you to explore your field, to get a hands-on feel for what can be an exciting career. It's an opportunity to observe and imagine yourself at work in the profession.

Public relations, for me, is influencing behavior through

strategic communication. In an internship you can look around and see firsthand how professionals apply their skills, knowledge and experience to influence behavior. They make plans to get people to support, to vote, to consider, to learn, to champion, to follow, to testify, to read, to buy, to trust, to invest, to listen, to become informed, to join, to leave alone, to contribute, to believe, to participate, to think, to work, to authorize, to accept, to welcome, to compromise, to accommodate, to cooperate, to wait, to attend, to decide and the list goes on and on and on. In an internship, you can learn how that is done. Just use your interpersonal skills to get others to show and teach you the fundamentals of persuasive communication.

Think of an internship not as someone's obligation to meet your expectations, but as your obligation to figure out how to use the internship opportunity to strengthen your skills to create, manage, connect, discuss, observe and have some fun in your profession.

Work hard at finding internships. Knock on doors. Get someone to let you in to explore what public relations is all about.

CHAPTER 12.

GET SUPERLATIVE RECOMMENDATION LETTERS

The classic way to get a letter of recommendation is simply to ask for one. You get it. Read it and say to yourself, "That's not a very strong endorsement." You wonder why the content is so superficial. If you want a strong, detailed, convincing recommendation, you need to plan certain actions in advance of asking for one. You need to give the endorser something to write about and that can't be done the day before you need the letter. You should plan your request at the beginning of the term. Decide how you want your endorser to describe your personality, character, performance. Focus on a few important attributes, then plan how you will make memorable impressions enough times to stick in the endorser's mind to show up in your recommendation letter. The strength of a recommendation letter you request depends entirely on you and how you present yourself to an endorser.

This advice will become perfectly clear when you read the list of attributes below. There are characteristics on the list that you think describe you, but how do you expect an endorser to assign them to you unless you demonstrate them? In addition, be helpful to the endorser; don't make the person have to look up information about which course, term, unique lessons learned, most outstanding assignment, final grade, etc. Review the list. Decide how would you like to be described:

♣ Shows remarkable intellectual curiosity ♣ Employs excellent critical thinking skills ♣ Does quality work consistently ♣ Arrives in class on time, every time ♣ Meets every deadline ♣ Follows the rules of classroom etiquette ♣ Takes pride in personal appearance ♣ Uses good judgment ♣ Has commendable personal values, especially honesty and integrity ♣ Is a team player, respected by colleagues ♣ Is flexible, adaptable, resilient, and adheres to professional ethics ♣ Relates respectfully to people of all ages ♣ Has an aspiring outlook ♣ Is an outstanding researcher, editor, writer and problem solver ♣ Learns quickly, is energetic, self-motivated ♣ Makes excellent use of class time.

CHAPTER 13.

INTERNSHIPS, ENTRY JOBS AND THE MATTER OF PAY

Here's some straight talk to put the whole matter of pay into perspective. Before you accept an offer for an internship or job, calculate your basic financial needs (i.e. housing, car, food, loan payments, etc.) Can you afford to get along with an unpaid internship? Can you afford to get along on a job salary that barely qualifies for food stamps?

Frankly, I think employers should be shamed of their justifications that put anyone into these situations. Some employers even break the law by billing a client regular business rates for work done by an intern who is working for nothing. Disgraceful!

Some interns get saddled with so much work that the job should be called an apprenticeship, like ones registered with the U.S. Department of Labor. How much money can an apprentice earn? Apprentices earn competitive wages, a paycheck from day one and incremental raises as skill levels increase. The average wage for a fully proficient worker who completes an apprenticeship translates to approximately $50,000 annually. Apprentices who complete their program earn approximately $300,000 more over their career than non-apprenticeship participants. Some might say this is comparing apples with oranges. Others might say that the profession should treat interns with more respect in substance and pay.

In addition to pay, here's what interns deserve in the substance of internships:

1. major responsibilities;
2. chances to perform;
3. trust to take direction, learn, deliver results;
4. resources necessary to do commendable work;
5. guidance enabling success;
6. high pay allowing interns to focus exclusively on the job;
7. employers worthy of having the fresh ideas, skills

and talents of interns.

As an intern, stand your ground, negotiate, resist letting anyone take advantage of your entry-level status. An employer should feel fortunate to have you on board.

CHAPTER 14.

YOUR PORTFOLIO PRESENTATION IS DUE!

Where do I begin?

Presenting a portfolio of your work is one of four job-seeking opportunities to make your qualifications irresistible to prospective employers. In addition to a portfolio, you have a cover letter, resume and interview.

Cheer up. This can be fun when you start early. The tactics in this presentation will distinguish you above all other candidates.

IMPRESSION

Appear before the interviewer in appropriate attire with your portfolio, ready to present, all else out of sight, including electronic devices.

Rehearse with a friend making first impressions in 7 seconds, looking:

- Friendly
- Confident
- Relaxed
- Genuine

CONTROL

You are the presenter. Take charge. You're in the spotlight. The interviewer will welcome your initiative.

Do not hand your portfolio materials to the interviewer to thumb through randomly. Politely hold on to your stuff! It's your show. Turn pages and point to items you have selected in advance. Mark with stickies. Use items to tout your skills. Tell why they should be of interest to the interviewer. Research, writing, editing, proofreading are skills highly desired by employers and should not be taken for granted.

Engage the interviewer. Encourage discussion. Show that you know how to listen.

RESULTS

Select one item in your portfolio that enables you to tell a story. Briefly explain a problem. Tell how it was solved with your involvement. Describe the solution. Use the words *results* and *measurable* more than once.

Point to other examples of solving problems, seizing opportunities and meeting challenges, always getting measureable results.

PRESENTATION

Plan your presentation.

Outline your plan.

Determine content and the order in which you will present it.

Rehearse your presentation with a friend as an audience. Ask your friend for help in refining the presentation in these areas:

- Voice projection (and personality)
- Rate of speech (confident, deliberate; not rapid fire and nervous)
- Persona (credibility, that you know what you're talking about)
- Clarity (plain talk, as in personal conversation)
- Tone (attitude)
- Pitch (varied)

- Energy (lean toward interviewer)
- Enthusiasm
- Emotion (that you can feel it and show it)
- Smiles (sincere, genuine)
- Humor
- Engagement (that you can talk and listen.)
- Crisp (sound bytes; no lengthy explanations)
- Positive statements (no qualifiers, excuses, apologies for anything)

SUMMARIZE

"So, my portfolio shows my skills in 15 different forms of PR writing."

"My portfolio shows that I pay great attention to detail."

"My portfolio shows that I always aim for measureable results."

"My portfolio shows…

CONCLUDE

If you really want the job, tell the interviewer: "This place feels right to me. I like the people. I like the work you do. I want to work here." Say that to others you meet.

Never walk away leaving the interviewer wondering about your interest. Offering a job is a risk to the interviewer, who doesn't want to be criticized for investing an organization's time and money in someone who quits after a month or two.

If you have reservations about the job, just be polite, but say something: "Thank you for taking an interest in me and my work."

Go for it!

CHAPTER 15.

ADD LEADERSHIP, RATHER THAN MEMBERSHIPS, TO YOUR RESUME

Turn memberships into evidence of your ability to recruit and build a multifaceted human effort, like a campaign, a not-for-profit project, a rally, forming of an online network, etc. Organizing people takes more than a simple, single solicitation. It takes leadership. Give an example of having organized people around a purpose-driven activity, and be able to explain how such an effort required you to lead, communicate and welcome.

Lead

Choose a cause or organization or create one. Volunteer to handle membership, or to be an officer with responsibilities for recruiting members. Win the trust and respect of potential members. Lead with warmth and competence.

Communicate

Commit yourself to a critical communication rule: Always put "we" before "I". Even candidates for the position of president of the United States have had to be coached to do that. Voters, in this example, want to be included as members of a democratic society. Always refer to members as "we," never as "they." "We" unifies, "they" divides.

Welcome

People join an organization because its purpose resonates with their interest and they believe that they can benefit from associating with it and contributing to its mission. To capture their interest, make them feel welcome. Help them find meaningful opportunities for their participation and recognize the value of their work, frequently.

When you join organizations, find a way to participate that gives you not just something to add to a list of activities, but tangible evidence of your ability to lead.

CHAPTER 16.

ANSWER THE TOUGH JOB INTERVIEW QUESTIONS

Employers fill jobs because their organizations have specific needs. In preparing answers to the following interview questions, think of what is behind employers' reasons for asking each question. For example, when an employer asks, "Where would you like to be in your career five years from now?" the employer is thinking of what it will cost to train you and how long you will make the investment worthwhile. An answer like, "I hope to have a law degree by then," would eliminate you as a job candidate.

Here is another example: if an employer asked, "Would you like to work here and, if so, when could you start?" you would be scratched as a candidate if you answered: "Oh yes, I would like to work here; I could start when I return from Europe".

1. What is public relations?

2. What brings you to our organization?

3. In what ways can you support the work of our staff?

4. What skills do you think are most important in PR? Explain why?

5. Why is it important to write in AP journalistic style?

6. What are your professional weaknesses?

7. What are some weaknesses of the PR profession?

8. Where would you like to be in your career five years from now?

9. How do you feel about traveling away from home on business trips?

10. Finish this statement about using electronic devices: "When I'm with a client, I would never…"

11. What would you advise a client about use of the social media?

12. Will I find spelling or grammatical errors in your portfolio?

13. What one thing do you think makes an event memorable?

14. How do you feel about being at work at eight o'clock every morning?

15. What do you think would be competitive pay for this job?

16. If you decided, "I deserve a break today," what would you do on your break?

17. How might you treat clients of older generations differently than those closer to your generation? Explain.

18. Tell me about a special event that you helped with?

19. What questions do you have about working here?

20. Would you like to work here and, if so, when could you start?

CHAPTER 17.

HOW TO INTERVIEW A PROSPECTIVE EMPLOYER

How do you feel about entering today's job market? What do you think your chances are of finding employers who will treat you with total respect, genuine appreciation for what you have to offer, and pay for the true value of your work?

There are many good employers. But they will be harder to find in a country that is influenced on all digital platforms by a continuing display of disrespect for the law, institutional norms, morality, ethnicity and civility. In place of courage, people in prominent positions are showing blind allegiance to ideologies at any cost. They are letting greed for money and power dominate human goals and ambitions, and publicly condoning the erosion of integrity. Hopefully, this dark cloud will pass. Meanwhile, it's a good time to break out of the job interviewing box.

It's time to turn the tables. Start interviewing employers! You have worked hard earning a college degree. You deserve an employer who will do more than provide a job. You deserve an employer who will add to your quality of life.

How do you do that? It is unlikely that every job seeker will be able to meet face to face with employers. But asking the right questions of employer representatives will reveal what you want to know about the employer and those who lead the organization.

Just wait for the proverbial question that comes up in every job interview: "What questions do you have?" This is your cue to take over the interview and dig into the heart and soul of the organization and its leaders.

Start asking about the employer's traits of integrity...

About your (chief executive officer or director)...

- shows total respect for everyone, regardless of pay grade?
- surrounds self with honest people?
- regarded as an honest person?
- known for keeping commitments to employees, customers, clients, investors, to everyone?
- trusted to tell the truth in every situation?
- shows compassion for others in need?
- gives people the benefit of the doubt?
- knows what it means to be humble?
- chooses to do the right thing in difficult situa-

tions?

- cares about the environment? About the community?

- makes thoughtful, not snap judgements?

- cares more about facts than optics?

- takes an interest in other people's opinions?

- trusts and works well with staff?

- knows the difference between confidence and arrogance?

- can admit when wrong and apologize?

- truthful when saying, You can count on it?

- shows kindness that is always genuine?

- considered moral and ethical?

Integrity, comprising the traits above, is a fundamental value employers seek in employees. What about employers? What do they expect of themselves? That is important to know because an employer can have a major effect on your quality of life. Interview the leader. Choose wisely.

CHAPTER 18.

WHY DID YOU BRING AN AP STYLEBOOK TO THIS INTERVIEW?

So, tell me why you brought an AP stylebook to this job interview. The answer to this question from a student to a prospective employer was that she was meticulous about writing in journalistic style and wanted to ensure that she made no errors on anything she was asked to write as part of the interview. She thought creatively about the meeting and made a stunning impression on the prospective employer. Writing is the most important skill in public relations. Writing in journalistic style is essential.

To help you learn AP style, this presentation identifies 126 items from the AP Stylebook that relate especially to public relations writing. They are arranged in 10 quizzes, each followed by an answer sheet. This is also an opportunity to learn standard editing marks, also found in the stylebook. Use standard editing marks to correct style errors in the quizzes.

AP Quiz 1

Edit the following for AP style using appropriate editing marks.

1. We attended a historic event.
2. I have a bachelor's degree in journalism.
3. It was arranged by Department Chairman Jeffrey Oliver.
4. The game will effect the standings.
5. Let's meet at 10pm.
6. Anyone of them may speak out.
7. Sally is the senator's aid.
8. Everyone from the department attended accept Stacy Thurston who was in New York preparing for a job interview.
9. Everyone thought it was alright to have the event on campus.

10. The speaker, George Fowler, is an alumnus of the university.

AP Quiz 1 ANSWERS

1. We attended a historic event. OK

2. I have a bachelor's degree in journalism. OK

3. It was arranged by Department Chairman Jeffrey Oliver. (department)

4. The game will effect the standings. (affect)

5. Let's meet at 10pm. (10 p.m.)

6. Anyone of them may speak out. (any one)

7. Sally is the senator's aid. (aide)

8. Everyone from the department attended accept Stacy Thurston who was in New York preparing for a job interview. (except)

9. Everyone thought it was alright to have the event on campus. (all right)

10. The speaker, George Fowler, is an alumnus of the university. OK

AP Quiz 2

Edit the following for AP style using appropriate editing marks.

1. Shannon plans to stay for a while.

2. He is the asst. dean responsible for student housing.

3. Molly left the department since she has no interest in the case.

4. Allison Lind is the first woman to serve on the Board of Directors.

5. That was defense attorney Perry Mason.

6. The capitol of Oregon is Salem.

7. The reference is found in Chapter 2.

8. He is a member of the Democratic party.

9. She had 35 cents in change.

10. The complaint went all the way to the headquarters and was read by chairwoman Florence Calvo.

AP Quiz 2 ANSWERS

1. Shannon plans to stay for a while. OK

2. He is the asst. dean responsible for student housing. (assistant)

3. Molly left the department since she has no interest in the case. (because)

4. Allison Lind is the first woman to serve on the Board of Directors. (board of directors)

5. That was defense attorney Perry Mason. OK

6. The capitol of Oregon is Salem. (capital)

7. The reference is found in Chapter 2. OK

8. He is a member of the Democratic party. (Party)

9. She had 35 cents in change. OK

10. The complaint went all the way to the headquar-

ters and was read by chairwoman Florence Calvo. (Chairwoman)

AP Quiz 3

Edit the following for AP style using appropriate editing marks.

1. With revenue of $27.5 billion, an increase of 14.5 percent over 1998, the Company has achieved 67 consecutive years of sales increases.

2. We will continue to focus our energies on building our business through internal development combined with selective acquisitions that compliment and strengthen our market or technological position.

3. Select the correct dateline(s): (a) BRUSH PRAIRIE, Wash.—January 22, 2002 (b) SEATTLE—January 22, 2002—

4. He is 5 feet 6 inches tall.

5. A storm system that developed in the midwest is spreading eastward.

6. The United States is comprised of 50 states.

7. In the United States, Congress refers to the U.S. Senate and House of Representatives.

8. That might have been true in the '80s.

9. The office is north of the plaza.

10. The objective is to (convince OR persuade) the target audience to accept new rules.

AP Quiz 3 ANSWERS

1. With revenue of $27.5 billion, an increase of 14.5 percent over 1998, the Company has achieved 67 consecutive years of sales increases. (company)

2. We will continue to focus our energies on building our business through internal development combined with selective acquisitions that compliment and strengthen our market or technological position. (complement)

3. Select the correct dateline(s): (a) BRUSH PRAIRIE, Wash.—January 22, 2002 (b) SEATTLE—January 22, 2002 (BOTH ARE CORRECT)

4. He is 5 feet 6 inches tall. OK

5. A storm system that developed in the midwest is spreading eastward. (Midwest)

6. The United States is comprised of 50 states. (composed)

7. In the United States, Congress refers to the U.S. Senate and House of Representatives. OK

8. That might have been true in the '80s. OK

9. The office is north of the plaza. OK

10. The objective is to (convince OR persuade) the target audience to accept new rules. (persuade)

AP Quiz 4

Edit the following for AP style using appropriate editing marks:

1. Steps were taken to insure accuracy.

2. Erin will look farther into the mystery.

3. We can see about 2/3rds of the picture.

4. He works full time.

5. They planned a fund raising campaign because fund raising requires a planned effort.

6. Jim was chosen to be emcee for the program.

7. He walked 4 miles or was it fifteen miles?

8. Every one of the clues was worthless.

9. Use my email address.

10. She goes to work every day.

AP Quiz 4 ANSWERS

1. Steps were taken to insure accuracy. (ensure)

2. Erin will look farther into the mystery. (further)

3. We can see about 2/3rds of the picture. (two-thirds)

4. He works full time. OK

5. They planned a fund raising campaign because fund raising requires a planned effort. (fund-raising)

6. Jim was chosen to be emcee for the program. (master of ceremonies)

7. He walked 4 miles or was it fifteen miles? (15)

8. Every one of the clues was worthless. OK

9. Use my email address. (e-mail)

10. She goes to work every day. (OK)

AP Quiz 5

Edit the following for AP style using appropriate editing marks:

1. We are operating our business in greater Portland.

2. You will find the information on the university's homepage.

3. It's time to input the data.

4. The name is in the data base.

5. We searched the worldwide web.

6. She graduated from the university.

7. Consider all of this to be high-tech.

8. You can send me an email message.

9. I login to my computer.

10. She is a member of the U.S. house of representatives.

AP Quiz 5 ANSWERS

1. We are operating our business in greater Portland. (Greater)

2. You will find the information on the university's homepage. (home page)

3. It's time to input the data. (enter)

4. The name is in the data base. (database)

5. We searched the worldwide web. (Web for World Wide Web)

6. She graduated from the university. OK

7. Consider all of this to be high-tech. OK

8. You can send me an email message. (OK)

9. I login to my computer. (log in)

10. She is a member of the U.S. house of representatives. (House of Representatives)

AP Quiz 6

Edit the following for AP style using appropriate editing symbols:

1. I plan to work irregardless of the holiday.

2. Its about time its name was changed.

3. Thomas Blanchard Jr. was guest speaker.

4. I will lay the book on the table.

5. We will win in the long term. He has a long-term assignment.

6. We are going to the Hawaiian islands.

7. Have you seen "Time" magazine?

8. He wrote six memorandums about it yesterday.

9. The news media is resisting government control.

10. The deadline is 12 midnight.

AP Quiz 6 ANSWERS

1. I plan to work irregardless of the holiday. (regardless)

2. Its about time its name was changed. (It's)

3. Thomas Blanchard Jr. was guest speaker. OK – NO COMMA

4. I will lay the book on the table. OK

5. We will win in the long term. He has a long-term assignment. OK

6. We are going to the Hawaiian islands. (Islands)

7. Have you seen "Time" magazine? (Time magazine)

8. He wrote six memorandums about it yesterday. OK

9. The news media is resisting government control. (media are)

10. The deadline is 12 midnight. (midnight)

AP Quiz 7

Edit the following for AP style using appropriate editing marks:

1. You won $3,000,000.00.

2. He was born on January 20, 1827.

3. Over 25 students attended the event.

4. Dunn and Noble received special recognition. David Dunn and Jean Noble were the first recipients of the trophy.

5. Ms. Jean Noble, Ms. Alice Wentworth and Ms.

Gloria Dinglewert registered a complaint with the head of the department.

6. It is multi-colored with a rough texture.

7. Everything is OK.

8. No body was available to keep order.

9. We will try reaching the party 9 times.

10. Did you know that it had ocured?

AP Quiz 7 ANSWERS

1. You won $3,000,000.00. ($3 million)

2. He was born on January 20, 1827. (Jan.)

3. Over 25 students attended the event. (More than)

4. David Dunn and Jean Noble received special recognition. David Dunn and Jean Noble were the first recipients of the trophy. (Delete first names in second use.)

5. Ms. Jean Noble, Ms. Alice Wentworth and Ms. Gloria Dinglewert registered a complaint with the head of the department. (correct)

6. It is multi-colored with a rough texture. (multicolored)

7. Everything is OK. OK

8. No body was available to keep order. (Nobody)

9. We will try reaching the party 9 times. (nine)

10. Did you know that it had ocured? (occurred)

AP Quiz 8

Edit the following for AP style using appropriate editing symbols:

1. You will find the information on Page 11.

2. She works part time.

3. The teacher said 60 per cent was a failing grade.

4. We have a meeting at 10am tomorrow.

5. For more information, contact professor Jim Van Leuven.

6. You need to talk to Atlanta Braves Owner Ted Turner.

7. Keep the list structure paralel.

8. Thousands of persons attended the fair.

9. The principle reason for this action is unknown.

10. We will conduct a press conference.

AP Quiz 8 ANSWERS

1. You will find the information on Page 11. OK

2. She works part time. OK

3. The teacher said 60 per cent was a failing grade. (percent)

4. We have a meeting at 10am tomorrow. (10 a.m.)

5. For more information, contact professor Jim Van Leuven. OK

6. You need to talk to Atlanta Braves Owner Ted Turner. (owner)

7. Keep the list structure paralel. (parallel)

8. Thousands of persons attended the fair. (people)

9. The principle reason for this action is unknown. (principal)

10. We will conduct a press conference. (news conference)

AP Quiz 9

Edit the following for AP style using appropriate editing symbols:

1. The problem did not reoccur.

2. We will meet in Room 211.

3. This class will be offered in the fall quarter.

4. John Jones is the man that helped me.

5. I have studied the style book.

6. She went to Madison Elementary School.

7. George was born in the State of Washington.

8. We saw the program on television station WTEV.

9. We went their for dinner.

10. The kidnappers set a 9am deadline.

AP Quiz 9 ANSWERS

1. The problem did not reoccur. (recur)

2. We will meet in Room 211. OK

3. This class will be offered in the fall quarter. OK

4. John Jones is the man that helped me. (who)

5. I have studied the style book. (stylebook)

6. She went to Madison Elementary School. OK

7. George was born in the State of Washington. (state of Washington)

8. We saw the program on television station WTEV. OK

9. We went their for dinner. (there)

10. The kidnappers set a 9am deadline. (9 a.m.)

AP Quiz 10

Edit the following for AP style using appropriate editing symbols:

1. A total of 600 students came to hear Hannah's speech.

2. This quiz counts towards the 263 entries we had to learn in the AP Stylebook.

3. Kristen will be on a TV talk show in Portland this weekend.

4. The program that Gabrielle is directing is now under way.

5. 2002 was a very good year for Sarah.

6. We are citizens of the US.

7. The best source is the Whitepaper on ethics.

8. The trend originated in the 1960's.

9. It is necessary to include a zip code and, in this

case, use New York, NY, 10020.

10. The launch will begin in 10 hrs. and 23 min.

AP Quiz 10 ANSWERS

1. A total of 600 students came to hear Hannah's speech. OK

2. This quiz counts towards the 263 entries we had to learn in the AP Stylebook. (toward)

3. Kristen will be on a TV talk show in Portland this weekend. OK

4. The program that Gabrielle is directing is now under way. OK

5. 2002 was a very good year for Sarah. OK

6. We are citizens of the US. (U.S.)

7. The best source is the Whitepaper on ethics. (white paper)

8. The trend originated in the 1960's. (1960s)

9. It is necessary to include a zip code and, in this case, use New York, NY 10020. (ZIP code for Zoning Improvement Plan and no comma after NY)

10. The launch will begin in 10 hrs. and 23 min. (hours minutes)

CHAPTER 19.

INFLUENCE PROSPECTIVE EMPLOYERS TO HIRE YOU

So much advice given for seeking employment focuses on the job candidate, when it should focus more on the interests and needs of potential employers. After all, employers go to the job market not to provide opportunities, but to fill needs. This chapter shows how to orient and integrate a cover letter, resume, portfolio and interview to address the needs and interests of prospective employers.

You can call a job an opportunity, but you should understand that it is a serious call for help. Before a job can be offered, hiring must be authorized within an organization. A need must be justified. The job must be described in detail. It must be ranked by criteria with all others. Ranking sets a salary range plus 30 percent or more for medical, vacation and other benefits. Only then can a job be announced by word-of-mouth, advertising, and various electronic means.

FOUR WAYS TO INFLUENCE PROSPECTIVE EMPLOYERS

As a job candidate, you have four ways to influence prospective employers: 1) cover letter; 2) resume; 3) interview; and 4) portfolio. Common practice is to develop each one separately. Common practice also is focusing everything on the job candidate and too little on the prospective employer's job needs. To illustrate with exaggeration:

- MY objective
- MY major achievements
- MY experience
- MY education
- MY skills
- MY activities
- MY references

Your objective should be to provide prospective employers with information that makes hiring you irresistible. It means presenting the best of you and showing an interest in employer needs in everything you provide—cover letter, resume, interview responses and portfolio. Integrate your approach. Address employer interests and needs as you develop each element of the four job-seeking areas. Following are tips to guide your effort.

Cover letter tips to influence the employer

Write a cover letter not just to present yourself, but to show that you understand the employer's interests and needs and believe that you are a good candidate for the job. Before you begin writing your cover letter, broaden your perspective to see the interests and needs of a prospective employer.

What employers are looking for in prospective employees:

- a person who is technologically savvy
- fits right into the organization
- won't require remedial training
- has the skills to jump in and share the work
- is familiar with the organization's work
- energetic, enthusiastic
- in touch with the real world
- relates well to others
- requires minimal supervision
- eager and quick to learn
- takes initiative
- good work ethic

- good long-term investment; will be on board for a while
- driven by the positive kinds of motivation
- gathers information thoroughly and accurately and makes thoughtful decisions
- works well alone, as well as with others
- has skills for managing others, including outside services
- has positive behavioral traits
- self-confidence and ability to travel on business and manage expenses

Resume tips to influence employers

Candidate writes: My objective is to obtain a position in the field of public relations that enables me to apply my academic training and experience.

Employer would like: My objective is to be hired as a public relations staff assistant by XYZ, Inc., so that the company will have the support it needs and I will be able to put my experience and academic training to good use.

Candidate writes: Major Achievements —Account Executive, Campaigns Course, Spring 20??; Fundraising Chairman, Public Relations Student Society of America, 20??-20??

Employer would like: Achievements—Generated 100 sales leads for an actual client in my campaigns course as account executive, 20??; helped raise $1,000 for a charity as chair of the PRSSA chapter, 20?? – 20??

Candidate writes: Experience—Student Assistant, Tennessee Law Review, Knoxville, Tenn.—promoted subscriptions, billed and shipped large orders, assigned articles to editors, checked prices with printers, sent out letters of rejection and acceptance, and assisted with special events.

Employer would like: Experience—Student Assistant, Tennessee Law Review, Knoxville, Tenn.—learned persuasive direct mail techniques, how to freelance articles acceptable for publication, good customer relations practices, and methods for and planning successful special events.

Candidate writes: Experience—Hostess, Knoxville Center, Knoxville, Tenn.—organized special events, sold tickets, answered questions from fans and dealt with complaints.

Employer would like: Experience—Hostess, Knoxville Center, Knoxville, Tenn.—acquired effective interpersonal skills for catering to fans and handling complaints, learned how to organize special events, and how to properly manage budgets and account for ticket sales.

Candidate writes: Education—Bachelor's Degree, June 20??; University of Oregon, Eugene, Ore.; Major/Complementary Courses, Public Relations, GPA: 3.75.

Employer would like: Education—Major, Public Relations; Major/Complementary Courses, Public Relations, GPA XXX, Bachelor's Degree 20??; University of Oregon.

Candidate writes: Skills—understand and have sound knowledge of Microsoft Word, Publics, First Choice, Web Design, In-Design, PowerPoint, PhotoShop, Social Media; excellent interpersonal and communicative skills.

Employer would like: Skills—research, writing and editing; AP journalistic style, grammar, proofreading, strategic use of social media, interpersonal communication, proficiency in all major software programs.

Candidate writes: References—available on request.

Employer would like: References—Tom Hagley, Senior Instructor of Public Relations, University of Oregon, School of Journalism & Communication, (cell) 111 222-3333.

NOTE: There are differences of opinion about providing references. A rationale for providing a name and number is that if there are two or three equally good choices, an employer might like just to lift the phone and talk to someone, rather than contact three candidates, ask for references, wait for responses, call the references and eventually make a choice.

Job Interview Tips To Influence Prospective Employers

Before answering questions, think how to address what might be behind an interviewer's questions, for example:

- evidence of a strong work ethic
- curious interest in everything
- dedication to detail
- ability to take direction and follow through

- self confidence
- sense of humor
- trust to deliver on promises and not promise more than one can deliver
- willingness to travel
- attitude toward working overtime
- team player
- ability to work under pressure

More to consider in answering interview questions:

- Give short, but complete answers to questions
- Do not apologize, minimize, or qualify anything
- Turn on your energy field; be passionate
- Show that you can feel and show emotion
- Physically lean into your responses to questions
- Give the best performance of being yourself
- If you want the job, say so enthusiastically to everyone with whom you interview
- Show a desire to want to be helpful—one of the most appreciated qualities in the workplace
- Know that people who interview are on the look-out for reasons not to hire someone
- When asked about weaknesses, provide a positive response, for example, "I love to learn; sometimes I think I ask too many questions."
- Don't ask for favors: "Before I start, I'd like to go

to Europe."

- Present yourself as a good investment. Do not say, for example, "Eventually I'd like to learn culinary arts"

- Appreciate the employer's pressing need and desire to fill a position

- Be prepared to ASK questions "What do you like most about working here?" "How is the PR function organized?" "Is there room for a person to progress?" "What are the strengths and weaknesses of the PR function here?" "How can I be of most help you?" "How can I best support your staff ?" "How does senior management regard public relations?" "Are you satisfied with the budget authorized for PR?"

Portfolio tips to influence employers

First Impression

Practice making first impressions in 7 to 10 seconds. Rehearse with a friend. The image to project is:

- Friendly

- Confident

- Relaxed

- Genuine

- Appropriately attired

CONTROL

You are the presenter. Take charge, especially if the interviewer is slow in getting started. It's your show. You're in the spotlight. The interviewer is likely tired of the process, feels kind of stuck in a rut and will gladly welcome your initiative. Seize the opportunity. Do not hand over your portfolio materials for someone to thumb through randomly. Hold on to your stuff. Point to items you have selected in advance. Use them to tout your skills. Tell why they should be of interest to the interviewer. Research, writing, editing, proofreading are skills highly desired by employers and should not be taken for granted.

RESULTS

Select one item in your portfolio that enables you to tell a story. Briefly explain a problem. Tell how it was solved with your involvement. Describe the solution's results in measurable terms. Do this at least once in your presentation. Show that you are a problem-solver. Talk results!

PRESENTATION

Outline your presentation. Determine content and the order in which you will present it. Rehearse it with a friend as an audience. Ask your friend for help in refining it in these areas:

- Voice projection
- Rate of speech
- Clarity
- Tone (attitude)
- Pitch (varied)

- Energy

- Enthusiasm

- Smiles

- Humor

- Engagement

- Points in sound bytes

- Crisp

SUMMARIZE YOUR SKILLS

"So, my portfolio shows my skills in 15 different forms of PR writing." "My portfolio shows that I pay great attention to detail." "My portfolio shows that I always aim for results." "My portfolio shows…"

CONCLUDE YOUR PORTFOLIO PRESENTATION

If you really want the job, tell the interviewer–"This place feels right to me. I like the people. I like the work you do. I want to work here." Never walk away leaving the interviewer wondering about your interest. Offering a job is a risk to the interviewer, who doesn't want to be criticized for investing an organization's time and money in someone who quits after a month or two. If you have reservations about the job, just be polite, but say something–"Thank you for taking an interest in me and my work."

CHAPTER 20.

SHUD JOB INERVIEWS INCLOOD SPELLING TESTS?

Should job interviews include spelling tests?

Dana Milbank, a columnist for The Washington Post Writers Group, in a recent article, wrote that one might be tempted to say misspellings "are evidence of a lack of education or an indication that they [people who misspell words] are not so bright."

He goes on to write that "habitual sloppiness and recklessness [with spelling] might also be seen as "equal carelessness" in other areas of a person's work.

Throughout his column, Milbank uses President Trump's poor spelling to illustrate his points:

"The morning after his inauguration, Trump tweeted 'I am honered to serve you, the great American People, as your 45th President of the United States!'"

"Trump's tweet on Hillary Clinton included three misspellings in the space of 140 characters: 'Hillary Clinton should not be given national security briefings in that she is a lose cannon with extraordinarily bad judgement & insticts.'"

Trump labeled Sen. Marco Rubio, R-Tex., a "lightweight chocker" and "always a chocker" after the senator choked in a GOP presidential debate. "He attacked Sen. Ted Cruz, R-Tex., by tweeting: 'Big shoker! People do not like Ted.'"

"Trump also tweeted that Cruz 'will loose big to Hillary.'"

"Ridiculous became 'rediculus,' Phoenix became 'Phoneix' (a felicitous phonics failure), and many paid attention when Trump proclaimed that he was not 'bought and payed for.'"

Dana Milbank's email is: dana.milbank@washpost.com.

Another example: Trump tweet, December 10, 2018:

"Democrats can't find a "Smocking" Gun tying the Trump campaign to Russia after James Comey's testimony. No "Smocking" Gun...No Collusion." That's because there was NO COLLUSION. So now the Dems go to a simple

private transaction, wrongly call it a campaign contribution,…"

Another example:

Mispelled Tickets Issued for 'State of the Uniom' Address?

Sitting senators tweeted images of the misspelled tickets
on 29 January 2018.

CHAPTER 21.

POST YOUR ONLINE IMAGE WITH PURPOSE

Give your online image purpose.

I looked through hundreds of online thumbnail photos. Many fit a purpose for being on the Internet in a particular network. Many did not. The photos ranged in value from useful to useless.

I thought it would be worthwhile to describe what I saw to encourage others to assess the image their photos are projecting and determine whether or not their selection of images is aligned with the purpose of each of the networks they have joined. In so many cases, images are totally out of character with the purpose of a particular network.

No need to get nervous. I'm not going to show, for obvious reasons, any of the people I chose for this impromptu review. But I am going to list descriptions that might or might not apply to you. If you can own up to a criticism, you will know what improvements you need to make. If your purpose is clear, you can just enjoy a complimentary observation. If your photo fits a description on the list and it's apparent that it is not in sync with your purpose and that of the host network, don't feel stuck with it. There is no reason to let yourself be held captive to a brand you have created for yourself. If a change would be beneficial, make it!

Descriptions of online images projected by individuals on various networks:

1. Side view, focuses on anything other than a face, failing to make the best use of thumbnail space with a full face head on view with a glimpse of personality

2. Purposely distorted image, cult-like, scary, crazy

3. Warm, genuine expression reflecting honesty and self-confidence

4. Five faces (in a thumbnail!) all competing for attention

5. Forced smile like a mask hiding some insecurity

6. Face size greatly reduced to show an environment or background

7. Intimidating, condescending, reading glasses perched on nose reflecting arrogance

8. Seductive pose

9. Expression of energy, enthusiasm, determination to achieve

10. Macho male or female model

11. Full-length view, like a model for men's suits

12. Hat, dark glasses, face down–hiding from who, or what?

13. Cold look, serious

14. Mean, untrustworthy

15. Smiling, happy, looking like a friend

16. Stoic, melancholic, lifeless

17. Face hidden behind sunglasses and camera

18. Face with meaningless sign, mark or logo

All expressions listed above were easy to find. They are in no way exclusive to any particular network; they are simply representative of images that appear online everywhere. Hopefully, this little study will prompt individuals to take time to assure themselves that the images they select are in line with a purpose and with that of networks in which they appear.

CHAPTER 22.

PROFESSIONAL DECORUM: WHAT DOES THAT MEAN?

The Washington Post

This photo of Kellyanne Conway on the couch in the Oval Office of The White House appeared in The Washington Post and for educational purposes clearly brings into view the matter of professional decorum. It is important to know how decorum relates to the public relations profession. Potential business is being lost over decorum. The notion that decorum is eroding and being replaced by new norms needs to be dispelled, because it isn't true. Decorum is taking on even greater importance with today's increasing attention to racial, gender and cultural diversity in the workplace.

A wave of revelations, investigations, accusations, prosecutions is sweeping the country in language that oftentimes is harsh, hurtful, rude, demeaning, intimidating, bullish, even childlike. This behavior is not going to supplant the requirements of a polite society. We have come a long way from throwing bones on the floor from the supper table. We have attained a life style in keeping with good taste, decency, civility, good form and customs. Irrational behavior is not a plague killing off human values faster than they can be protected. Businesses have lost clients over the attitude, appearance, manners, language and rudeness of staff members who act like they represent a new norm of doing business. This is bottom line evidence that decorum has not lost its importance.

Decorum doesn't pertain only to standards you set for yourself, with regard to how you appear, how you treat others, how you express yourself. Decorum is also being respectful of what others expect of your behavior in a polite society. Success favors people who strive to meet the requirements of a polite society.

CHAPTER 23.

PREPARE FOR A SURPRISE FEDERAL SEARCH AND SEIZURE OF YOUR FILES

Imagine! One morning you walk into your office and find yellow tape (like crime scene tape) threaded through the handles on every desk drawer and file cabinet. You discover that a representative of the U.S. Justice Department has searched and inventoried every one of your files and has left a copy of an inventory list in every drawer with a warning that everything is expected to stay in place for further review. Why? Why your office? You haven't participated in any illegal activity.

Here's how a public relations professional can get into

trouble, unwittingly, and why it is important to keep clean files. Can you think of anyone in an organization who has more and easier access to information than the PR person? Research is essential for preparing news announcements, speeches, white papers, executive correspondence, etc. Employees assume that the PR person is trusted by executive management to gather information verbally and in any media. As a result, the PR researcher often is given documents—studies, letters, reports, data sheets, and some with confidential information. The PR person, understandably feels privileged to have such information and could be tempted to make copies documents obtained from others for future writing assignments. Not a good idea.

In an investigation, everything is reviewed—all paper and electronic audio, video, text communication, including documents produced on copy machines and scanners. The best practice, especially with confidential information, is to use it and return it. The PR person has no way to know if research materials would withstand legal inspection. Keeping copies of materials could associate the PR person with potentially questionable activities of others within or outside the organization. Keep clean files for the unexpected.

Related advice on this subject

is about the absolute need to separate business and personal files. Today, jobs are not forever. When you least expect yours to be affected, it can get caught up in a rain of cuts, layoffs, pink slips, downsizing, reorganizing, bankruptcy, rumors of civil or criminal charges. Consider walking into your work space one morning and being met by an HR person handing you an empty cardboard box and offering to help you pack up your personal belongings. Under the watchful eye of the HR person, you start opening drawers and filling the box. You are told that all of the company's electronic devices—desktop, laptop, phone, etc. must remain in the work area, that passwords and codes have already been changed so you cannot access anything from home. Consider next that someone from Security escorts you out the door and onto the street. Consider feeling humiliated, fearful, and unable to think past the present.

You could have reduced some of the agony you would feel, had you kept your personal files separate from your business files. You could have eliminated the anger you would feel toward someone now able to look through your confiscated personal files, had you started out separating personal and business files. With a little foresight, proactive organization and continuing vigilance, you could be in a position at anytime, to walk out the door confidently, without looking back over your shoulder. Depending on how you felt about your job, you might even feel relieved, freed, liberated, unburdened and a little excited about starting a new chapter in your life. The tactic here is to take action now to separate your personal and business files and apply this advice to office and home.

CHAPTER 24.

OBSTRUCTING JUSTICE. WHO? ME!

Communication that you deliver publicly at the direction of your client or employer could get you indicted for obstruction of justice. It is in your interest as a professional communicator to recognize legal boundaries of this infraction to keep you from crossing them unwittingly.

Obstruction of justice is in the public eye today due to

the questionable behavior of highly visible public officials. It should be top of mind for professional communicators (spokespersons), especially those who think they
have protection from the law as innocent conveyors of
communication. They should think again.

Recall that Senator Sheldon Whitehouse (D-RI) warned
press secretary Sarah Huckabee Sanders that she could be
indicted for obstruction of justice. According to Whitehouse, Sanders may have placed herself in legal jeopardy
by being the White House point person in its actions to
publicly undermine the integrity of former FBI Director
James Comey.

Sen. Whitehouse, on MSNBC's "Hardball" with Chris
Matthews, explained there is a statute, 1504, in the
obstruction of justice statutes, that talks about attempts
to influence grand jurors. He said the questions for Sarah
Huckabee Sanders are, "Who asked you to do that? Who
told you to do that?" He continued to explain that once
you know who it is, you look to their motivation. And
if their motivation was to poison the reputation of Jim
Comey with grand jurors, you've got another count in the
indictment.

Obstruction of justice is a criminal offense of interfering
with the (1) administration or process of law, (2) with-
holding material information or giving false testimony, or
(3) harming or intimidating a juror, witness, or officer of
law.

The range of situations wherein a person can face
an obstruction of justice charge is wide. Therefore, so too

are the penalties for an obstruction of justice conviction. A typical obstruction of justice penalty can be anywhere from a fine (misdemeanor), to 10 years in prison (felony).

CHAPTER 25.

THINK NOW ABOUT TEACHING PUBLIC RELATIONS LATER

An outstanding classroom public relations team

No matter where you stand in your career, there are actions you can take now to prepare for teaching public relations, if that's what you might be thinking about doing in the future. Act now to keep opportunities from slipping through your fingers, only to exclaim later, "Why didn't I think of that!"

First, you need to fully appreciate the value of professional practice to an educator. A full-time instructor could be required, for example, to teach two different courses a week for 12 weeks. The scholar, with no professional experience, must develop lesson plans for some 96 hours of instruction based on information from textbooks, trade and academic publications, conferences, and other bodies of knowledge.

I can tell you from personal experience that an instructor with years of professional practice can converse freely, confidently and comfortably before a class of a dozen students to a lecture room of hundreds. But how does a person with work experience fill 96 or more hours of class time with instruction? That question takes us to the point of this post: It's not too late to prepare for teaching public relations.

As a practitioner, you have access to a treasure trove of teaching resources. Start collecting and saving them, even if you just have remote thoughts of eventually teaching PR. As allowable, set aside speeches, memos, slide shows, video clips, plans, proposals, news clippings, articles, presentations, audio and/or video recordings of meetings, protests, crisis situations, all matter of problem-solving situations. If you someday decide to teach, you will be so glad that you came across this advice.

PART III.

TACTICS TO EXCEL IN CLASS AND AT WORK

CHAPTER 26.

WHY PUBLIC RELATIONS PLANS GET REJECTED AND A PATHWAY FORWARD

Public relations plans and proposals get rejected because they confuse plan reviewers. For example, a plan reviewer says, "I thought this was the objective, but now you call it a goal." Unfortunately, too many PR practitioners cannot distinguish a goal, from an objective, from a strategy, from a tactic.

Let's illustrate the cause of confusion with an example from a national award-winning public relations plan. It states the goal of the plan is "...to have the public adopt natural garden care by changing certain gardening behaviors." A goal should describe a desired, ultimate condition or state of being as though it has been achieved. (E.g. For the public to be practicing natural garden care). To say that the goal is "...to have the public adopt..." leaves the target audience in its current state, trying to adopt something. Further, "...to have the public adopt natural garden care..." tells <u>what</u> must be done, which is the role of an objective. The phrase "by changing certain gardening behaviors" tells <u>how</u> something must be done, which is the role of a strategy.

Writing winning plans and proposals is one of the profession's oldest and greatest weaknesses. Evidence of this self-inflicted condition is the fact that it has always been difficult to find plans that qualify for national award competition. The profession perpetuates the situation with practitioners' insistence that "This is the way it's done." The profession presumes that its plan writing is acceptable to clients and employers. However, plan reviewers do not have a collective voice to say, "No, this is want we want and this is how we want it." They make their respective opinions known by rejecting plans, some being polite about it and saying, "I don't think we're ready to do that."

The lesson here is that it is important to study the components of a plan and use them correctly. However, you will find books with differing definitions of a goal, objective, strategy and tactic, just as there are among practitioners. Yet, your awareness of the overhanging cloud of confused terms should increase your desire to do something to raise the quality of your plan writing. Following are rules for writing four of 10 components of a plan.

GOAL

A goal describes a desired, ultimate condition or state of being as though it has been achieved. For example: For residents of the township to be practicing natural lawn care.

OBJECTIVE

An objective describes **what** must be done to achieve a plan's goal. An objective is distinguished by starting with the infinitive "To," and must contain three parts (1) an action to be taken, (2) a receiver of the action or target audience, (3) a behavior that is desired of the receiver as a result of the action taken. Example: To educate residents of the township about the benefits of natural lawn care so they take measures to prevent contamination of area lakes and streams.

STRATEGY

A strategy describes **how**, in concept, an objective is to be accomplished. More than one strategy could be required to accomplish a single objective. Example: We will accomplish Objective #1 with an integrated program of online community engagement that enables township residents to interact with, create, and share web content rather than be passive recipients of content.

TACTICS

Tactics are detailed steps to carry out strategies. Tactics should begin with a strategic move rather than a communication tool. For example, notice that the Tactic A example below begins with a strategic move (attract visitors) rather than a communication tool (build a website) because there is nothing strategic about a list of communication tools. There should be tactics for each strategy.

Example tactics:

Tactic A – Attract visitors to an online community engagement website that enables them to learn about the lawn care program, ask questions, offer suggestions, volunteer to help, chat with others, sign up for special events, join and converse with teams and become excited about reaching out and sharing what they discovered with friends and neighbors.

Tactic B. Identify a select number of township influencers, whose names and email addresses have been obtained from homeowner associations, community service organizations, environment, gardening, recreation and outdoors clubs, and ask them to post about the lawn care program on all forms of social media with which they have accounts.

Tactic C. Work with bloggers who write about the environmental management of lakes and streams and bring them and their followers into the online community engagement program for broad, outside recognition and discussion of the township's natural lawn care activities.

Tactic D. Organize street parties, using the Internet, sponsored by natural lawn care products manufactures.

Tactic E. Conduct a contest for students and their affiliated schools to create the township's natural lawn care icon and show entries on the Internet site with background cartoon music as they are submitted and displayed and ultimately awarded prizes.

My personal experience in being presented with plans requiring corporate expenditures of thousands of dollars motivated me to write a textbook for teaching a university course in public relations problems and plan writing. *Writing Winning Proposals: Public Relations Cases* was produced in a third edition in 2018 with co-author Rebecca A. Gilliland, Professor of Communication and Director of the Public Relations Program at the University of Indianapolis. The text is written entirely from the perspective of plan reviewers showing what they want in plans and the way they want to get it.

CHAPTER 27.

HAVE YOU BEEN MANIPULATED BY RUSSIAN TROLLS?

Russian trolls manipulate how people think, behave and act.

Russian trolls might be closer to home than you think. Answer 12 questions presented in this chapter to determine if you have been or are being manipulated by the Russian-controlled International Research Agency (IRA).

At the IRA in Saint Petersburg, Russians are hired as "content managers" and turned into Internet trolls. They are looking for social and political U.S. activists to help them do their work. If you spend time creating an online identity for yourself, actively attracting an ever-increasing number of followers, you are making yourself vulnerable to Internet trolling. More than that, you could be falling under the influence of trolls dedicated to undermining the well-being of the country in which you live.

There is no secret here. These happenings were revealed in great detail by the U.S. Department of Justice. The only secret might be that you don't realize this could be happening to you. Unknowingly, you could be acting as an agent of chaos for the Russian government.

On Feb. 16, 2018, the U.S. Department of Justice charged the IRA with conspiring to impair, obstruct and defeat the lawful government functions of the United States by dishonest means in order to enable the IRA to interfere with U.S. political and electoral processes, including the 2016 U.S. presidential election. The IRA to this day, according to intelligence sources, continues to use devious, illegal means to manipulate the way U.S. persons think, feel, and act. A former Russian troll said publicly, "...for Americans, it appears it did work. They aren't used to this kind of trickery."

So how is it that you might have been or are being manipulated by Russian trolls—helping them carry out their operations of creating social divisions by causing disagreement and division around any social or political issues, like immigration and Islamophobia? Trolls do their work using stolen identities, communicating perfectly as English-speaking individuals. They pose online as U.S. opinion leaders. They are right at home in the U.S., so to speak, gathering intelligence from and exchanging views with real U.S. activists, using fake accounts on Facebook, Twitter, Instagram, Tumblr and YouTube.

To determine whether or not trolls have been or are in touch with you, answer the following questions.

1. Have you unknowingly provided information to anyone online who asked about social and political life in the U.S., intelligence that could be used by trolls to sharpen their skills at creating chaos? One U.S. person, for example, advised a troll posing as a U.S. person to focus on "purple states" and explained why.

2. Have you come across content on the Internet that describes incredibly well how you feel about an issue? Was the content so well crafted [by trolls] that it fortified your feelings to the point of being outraged beyond discussion at people who don't hold your view with the same intensity? The troll's aim in this case is not the issue; the aim is driving a deep wedge between people using issues. The approach is not a frontal assault, but rather working within individuals, intensifying feelings

of people on one side of an issue and doing the same with people on the other side of an issue, thereby creating great discord between individuals.

3. Have you found content online that seemed so outrageously truthful in support of your view that you couldn't wait to share it with friends and even all of your followers, not knowing that it was totally untruthful and intended by trolls to spread fake, destructive information to countless numbers of U.S. persons?

4. Have you visited social media sites, unknowingly themed and managed by trolls, such as Secured Borders, Blacktivist, United Muslims of America, Army of Jesus, South United, Heart of Texas—groups that have grown to hundreds of thousands of online followers?

5. Have you, unwittingly, followed troll-created and controlled Twitter accounts, such as Tennessee GOP that used the handle @TEN_GOP and amassed more than 100,000 followers.

6. Have you physically attended a rally because of persuasive content you found online that looked to be from a typical Internet site, not knowing that the entire event was created and sent into the country on private computers from Saint Petersburg? Trolls have been able to create a rally in one part of a state supporting one candidate and a rally in another part of a state supporting an opposing candidate.

7. Were you encouraged to bring anything to a rally, like protest signs and friends?

8. Were you nearly convinced by an Internet post that in a particular election the best choice was not to vote?

9. Were you attracted to certain sites during the 2016 U.S. presidential election? Trolls used fictitious online personas to interfere with the election. They engaged in operations primarily intended to communicate derogatory information about Hillary Clinton, to denigrate other candidates such as Ted Cruz and Marco Rubio, and to support Bernie Sanders and then-candidate Donald Trump.

10. Trolls pretended to have the same religious convictions as targeted users, and often promoted Biblical memes, including one that showed Clinton as Satan, with budding horns, arm-wrestling with Jesus, alongside the message, "'Like' if you want Jesus to win!" Did you press, Like?

11. Did you, unwittingly, follow the trolls' Twitter online social media accounts "March for Trump" and Facebook accounts "Clinton FRAUDation" or "Trumpsters United?"

12. Did you, as a member, volunteer, or supporter of the Trump Campaign communicate, unwittingly, about community outreach with trolls who were using false U.S. personas?

Your answers to the above 12 questions could enable you

to know whether or not you have been or are being manipulated by Internet trolls.

This chapter was written to raise awareness of cyber trolls lurking on the Internet with strategic operations to influence the way you think, feel and act. This knowledge can help protect you from being used for someone else's malicious and illegal efforts to destabilize this nation by intensifying existing divisions among people. Hopefully, you now have an even greater respect for "Internet content management" and the powerful influence it can have on people. You can better appreciate the essential need to pay attention to the personal side of managing social media content; that is thinking more about how you engage with information online, how it affects your emotions and actions, and how critically necessary it is for you to assess sources.

Trolls referred to in this chapter are Russians, many unemployed looking for work, lured into applying to job listings for "content managers," finding out later that they were intended from the beginning to be used as Internet trolls by the Russian-controlled International Research Agency referred to as the troll farm. The pay is attractive to many, about $700 a month, working 12-hour days, two days on, two days off.

In an interview with former trolls, The Washington Post asked what it's like inside the IRA building. The troll said, "Your first feeling…was that you were in some kind of factory that turned lying, telling untruths, into an industrial assembly line. The volumes were colossal. There were huge numbers of people, 300 to 400, and they were all writing absolute untruths."

The troll continued, "My untruths amounted to posting comments... I had to comment on the news. No one asked me my opinion. My opinions were already written for me, and I had to write in my own words what I was ordered to write." According to The Washington Post, the troll said that there were daily production norms, for example, 135 comments of 200 characters each. "You got a list of topics to write about," the troll said. "We had to make it look like we were not trolls but real people... Who really reads comments under news articles anyway? Especially when they were so obviously fake... But for Americans, it appears it did work. They aren't used to this kind of trickery... "

Cyber warfare is a big part of the future of nations. Cyber armies are springing up in countries everywhere. Fruzsina Eordogh, contributor to Forbes, wrote: "... the Kremlin's cyber soldiers aren't the only country running disinformation campaigns in the U.S. In fact, every country that has an adversarial stance with the United States has amassed at least hundreds of online propaganda warriors, mostly in the form of bots and fake accounts. An oxford study two years ago noted at least 30 nations were utilizing them. While most countries use their troll armies to police and influence their own citizens, some have already turned their attention to our shores as well as to our allies.

CHAPTER 28.

WHAT YOU SHOULD KNOW ABOUT CYBER WARFARE

Russian hackers are at work

This chapter presents details of how Russian hackers used and continue to use, the Internet to undermine the strength of the United States. It's important for you to know details of how the United States was hacked to fully appreciate that:

- without the rockets' red glare and bombs bursting in air, the public remained oblivious to a cyberattack that swept across the entire country;

- movement of the attack ran forcefully and silently beneath the surface causing currents of doubt, confusion, division, incivility, disrespect and other blameworthy behaviors;

- it was easy with social media to play on the human tendency of people to seek and associate with what they want to believe;

- the weapons of cyber warfare are virtually unlimited in the ways they can be developed, interconnected, aimed, fired, reloaded and resupplied;

- the anonymity of the attackers can be almost impenetrable;

- even when given evidence detailing an attack, the public does not have the background necessary to comprehend the dangers or enormity of its impact on human behavior;

- without public knowledge of cyber warfare, representative leaders of the country will have a difficult time obtaining funds to deal with the threat;

- as a professional communicator, making strategic use of social media, you are in a unique position to recognize evidence of cyber warfare, be a moral agent, and do what's right to protect others from destructive cyber activity.

The strategic use of social media is serious business. It can be likened to a certified electrician's use of lethal power, channeling it through interconnected devices, and running it through a variety of circuits to make things happen. You will see on the following pages extracts from the criminal indictment of Russian nationals how the use of social media power to influence human behavior can, like lethal electrical power, be strong and useful, harmful and destructive.

On Friday, February 16, 2018, Deputy Attorney General Rod Rosenstein announced that the special counsel, Robert Mueller, had indicted 13 Russian nationals and three Russian entities on charges that included conspiracy to defraud the United States, conspiracy to commit wire fraud and bank fraud, and aggravated identity theft.

Details extracted from the federal indictment on the following pages illustrate dramatically how the conspiracy was executed in seven areas: 1) intelligence gathering; 2) use of social media platforms; 3) use of computer infrastructure; 4) use of stolen U.S. identities; 5) actions targeting the 2016 presidential election; 6) political advertisements; and, 7) staging U.S. political rallies in the U.S.

The objective of the conspiracy was to impair, obstruct, and defeat lawful governmental functions of the United States by dishonest means to enable the defendants to interfere with U.S. political and electoral processes, including the 2016 U.S. presidential election.

MANNER AND MEANS OF THE CONSPIRACY

Intelligence-Gathering

Starting at least in or around 2014, the defendants and their co-conspirators began to track and study groups on U.S. social media sites dedicated to U.S. politics and social issues. To gauge the performance of various groups on social media sites, they tracked certain metrics, like the group's size, the frequency of content placed by the group, and the level of audience engagement with that content, such as the average number of comments or responses to a post. They also traveled, and attempted to travel, to the United States under false pretenses to collect intelligence for their interference operations.

To collect additional intelligence, they posed as U.S. persons and contacted U.S. political and social activists. For example, starting in or around June 2016, posing online as U.S. persons, they communicated with a real U.S. person affiliated with a Texas-based grassroots organization. During the exchange, they learned from the real U.S. person that they should focus their activities on "purple states," like Colorado, Virginia and Florida. After that exchange, they commonly referred to targeting "purple states" in directing their efforts.

Use of U.S. Social Media Platforms

Through fraud and deceit, they created hundreds of social media accounts and used them to develop certain fictitious U.S. personas into "leaders of public opinion" in the United States. They hired employees, referred to as "specialists," who were tasked to create social media accounts that appeared to be operated by U.S. persons. The specialists were divided into day-shift and night-shift hours and instructed to make posts in accordance with the appropriate U.S. time zone. They also circulated lists of U.S. holidays so that specialists could develop and post appropriate account activity. Specialists were instructed to write about topics germane to the United States, such as U.S. foreign policy and U.S. economic issues. Specialists were directed to create "political intensity through supporting radical groups, users dissatisfied with the social and economic situation and oppositional social movements."

They also created thematic group pages on social media sites, particularly on the social media platforms Facebook and Instagram. Their controlled pages addressed a range of issues, including: immigration (with group names including "Secured Borders"); the Black Lives Matter movement (with group names including "Blacktivist"); religion (with group names including "United Muslims of America" and "Army of Jesus"); and certain geographic regions within the United States (with group names including "South United" and "Heart of Texas"). By 2016, the size of many of their controlled groups had grown to hundreds of thousands of online followers.

Starting at least in or around 2015, they began to purchase advertisements on online social media sites to promote their controlled social media groups, spending thousands of U.S. dollars every month.

They also created and controlled numerous Twitter accounts designed to appear as if U.S. persons or groups controlled them. For example, they created and controlled the Twitter account "Tennessee GOP," which used the handle @TEN_GOP. The @TEN_GOP account falsely claimed to be controlled by a U.S. state political party. Over time, the@TEN_GOPaccount attracted more than 100,000 online followers.

To measure the impact of their online social media operations, they tracked the performance of content they posted over social media. They tracked the size of the online U.S. audiences reached through posts, different types of engagement with the posts (such as likes, comments, and reposts), changes in audience size, and other metrics. They received and maintained metrics reports on certain group pages and individualized posts.

They also regularly evaluated the content posted by specialists (sometimes referred to as "content analysis") to ensure they appeared authentic—as if operated by U.S. persons. Specialists received feedback and directions to improve the quality of their posts. They issued or received guidance on: ratios of text, graphics, and video to use in posts; the number of accounts to operate; and the role of each account (for example, differentiating a main account from which to post information and auxiliary accounts to promote a main account through links and reposts).

Use of U.S. Computer Infrastructure

To hide their Russian identities, they purchased space on computer servers located inside the United States to set up virtual private networks ("VPNs"). The defendants and their co-conspirators connected from Russia to the U.S.-based infrastructure by way of these VPNs and conducted activity inside the United States—including accessing online social media accounts, opening new accounts, and communicating with real U.S. persons—while masking the Russian origin and control of the activity.

They also registered and controlled hundreds of web-based email accounts hosted by U.S. email providers under false names so as to appear to be U.S. persons and groups. From these accounts, they registered or linked to online social media accounts to monitor them; posed as U.S. persons when requesting assistance from real U.S. persons; contacted media outlets to promote activities inside the United States and conducted other operations.

Use of Stolen U.S. Identities

In or around 2016, they used, possessed, and transferred, without lawful authority, the social security numbers and dates of birth of real U.S. persons without those persons' knowledge or consent. Using these means of identification, they opened accounts at PayPal, the digital payment service provider; created false means of identification, including fake driver's licenses; and posted on their controlled social media accounts using the identities of these U.S. victims. They also obtained, and attempted to obtain, false identification documents to use as proof of identity in connection with maintaining accounts and purchasing advertisements on social media sites.

Actions Targeting the 2016 U.S. Presidential Election

By approximately May 2014, they discussed efforts to

interfere in the 2016 U.S. presidential election. They began to monitor U.S. social media accounts and other sources of information about the 2016 U.S. presidential election.

By 2016, they used their fictitious online personas to interfere with the 2016 U.S . presidential election. They engaged in operations primarily intended to communicate derogatory information about Hillary Clinton, to denigrate other candidates such as Ted Cruz and Marco Rubio, and to support Bernie Sanders and then-candidate Donald Trump.

On or about February 10, 2016, they internally circulated an outline of themes for future content to be posted to their controlled social media accounts. Specialists were instructed to post content that focused on "politics in the USA" and to "use any opportunity to criticize Hillary and the rest (except Sanders and Trump; we support them)."

On or about September 14, 2016, in an internal review of their created and controlled Facebook group called "Secured Borders," an account specialist was criticized for having a "low number of posts dedicated to criticizing Hillary Clinton" and was told "it is imperative to intensify criticizing Hillary Clinton" in future posts. Their produced materials about the 2016 U.S. presidential election used election-related hashtags, including: " #Trump2016," "#TrumpTrain," "#MAGA," "#IWontProtectHilalry," and "#Hillary4Prison." They also established additional online social media accounts dedicated to the 2016 U.S. presidential election, including the Twitter account "March for Trump" and Facebook accounts "Clinton FRAUDation" and "Trumpsters United." They also used false U.S. personas to communicate with unwitting members, volunteers, and supporters of the Trump Campaign involved in local community outreach, as well as grassroots groups that supported then-candidate Trump. These individuals and entities at times distributed materials through their own accounts via retweets, reposts, and similar means. They then monitored the propagation of content through such participants.

In or around the latter half of 2016, through their controlled personas, they began to encourage U.S. minority groups not to vote in the 2016 U.S. presidential election or to vote for a third-party U.S. presidential candidate. On or about October 16, 2016, they used their controlled Instagram account "Woke Blacks" to post the following message: "[A] particular hype and hatred for Trump is misleading the people and forcing Blacks to vote Hillary. We cannot resort to the lesser of two devils. Then we'd surely be better off without voting AT ALL." On or about November 3, 2016, they purchased an advertisement to promote a post on their controlled Instagram account "Blacktivist" that read in part: "Choose peace and vote for Jill Stein. Trust me, it's not a wasted vote."

By in or around early November 2016, they used their controlled "United Muslims of America" social media accounts to post anti-vote messages such as: "American Muslims [are] boycotting elections today, most of the American Muslim voters refuse to vote for Hillary Clinton because she wants to continue the war on Muslims in the middle east and voted yes for invading Iraq."

Starting in or around the summer of 2016, they also began to promote allegations of voter fraud by the Democratic Party through their fictitious U.S. personas and groups on social media. They purchased advertisements on Facebook to further promote the allegations. On or about August 4, 2016, they began purchasing advertisements that promoted a post on the their controlled Facebook account "Stop A.I." The post alleged that "Hillary Clinton has already committed voter fraud during the Democrat Iowa Caucus." On or about August 11, 2016, they posted that allegations of voter fraud were being investigated in North Carolina on their controlled Twitter account@TEN_GOP. On or about November 2, 2016, they used the same account to post allegations of "#VoterFraud by counting tens of thousands of ineligible mail in Hillary votes being reported in Broward County, Florida."

Political Advertisements

From at least April 2016 through November 2016, while concealing their Russian identities through false personas, they began to produce, purchase, and post advertisements on U.S. social media and other online sites expressly advocating for the election of then-candidate Trump or expressly opposing Clinton. They did not report their expenditures to the Federal Election Commission, or register as foreign agents with the U.S. Department of Justice. To pay for the political advertisements, they established various Russian bank accounts and credit cards, often registered in the names of fictitious U.S. personas they created and used on social media. They also paid for other political advertisements using PayPal accounts.

Staging U.S. Political Rallies in the United States

Starting in approximately June 2016, they organized and coordinated political rallies in the United States. To conceal the fact that they were based in Russia, they promoted these rallies while pretending to be U.S. grassroots activists who were located in the United States but unable to meet or participate in person. They did not register as foreign agents with the U.S. Department of Justice.

To build attendance for the rallies, they promoted the events through public posts on their false U.S. persona social media accounts. In addition, they contacted administrators of large social media groups focused on U.S. politics and requested that they advertise the rallies.

In or around late June 2016, they used the Facebook group "United Muslims of America" to promote a rally called "Support Hillary. Save American Muslims" held on July 9, 2016, in the District of Columbia. they recruited a real U.S. person to hold a sign depicting Clinton and a quote attributed to her stating "I think Sharia Law will be a powerful new direction of freedom." Within three weeks, on or about July 26, 2016, they posted on the same Facebook page that Muslim voters were "between Hillary Clinton and a hard place."

In or around June and July 2016, they used the Facebook group "Being Patriotic," the Twitter account @March_for_Trump, and other controlled accounts to organize two political rallies in New York. The first rally was called "March for Trump" and held on June 25, 2016.

The second rally was called "Down with Hillary" and held on July 23, 2016.

In or around June through July 2016, they purchased advertisements on Facebook to promote the "March for Trump" and "Down with Hillary" rallies. They used false U.S. personas to send individualized messages to real U.S. persons to request that they participate in and help organize the rally. To assist their efforts, through false U.S. personas, they offered money to certain U.S. persons to cover rally expenses.

On or about June 5, 2016, while posing as a U.S. grassroots activist, they used the account @March_for_Trump to contact a volunteer for the Trump Campaign in New York. The volunteer agreed to provide signs for the "March for Trump" rally.

In or around late July 2016, they used the Facebook group "Being Patriotic," the Twitter account @March_for_Trump, and other false U.S. personas to organize a series of coordinated rallies in Florida. The rallies were collectively referred to as "Florida Goes Trump" and held on August 20, 2016.

In or around August 2016, they used false U.S. personas to communicate with Trump Campaign staff involved in local community outreach about the "Florida Goes Trump" rallies. They purchased advertisements on Facebook and Instagram to promote the "Florida Goes Trump" rallies. They also used false U.S. personas to contact multiple grassroots groups supporting then-candidate Trump in an unofficial capacity. Many of these groups agreed to participate in the "Florida Goes Trump" rallies and serve as local coordinators. They also used false U.S. personas to ask real U.S. persons to participate in the " Florida Goes Trump" rallies. They asked certain of these individuals to perform tasks at the rallies.

For example, they asked one U.S. person to build a cage on a flatbed truck and another U.S. person to wear a costume portraying Clinton in a prison uniform. They paid these individuals to complete the requests. After the rallies in Florida, they used false U.S. personas to organize and coordinate U.S. political rallies supporting then-candidate Trump in New York and Pennsylvania. They used the same techniques to build and promote these rallies as they had in Florida, including: buying Facebook advertisements; paying U.S. persons to participate in, or perform certain tasks at, the rallies; and communicating with real U.S. persons and grassroots organizations supporting then-candidate Trump.

After the election of Donald Trump in or around November 2016, they used false U.S. personas to organize and coordinate U.S. political rallies in support of then president-elect Trump, while simultaneously using other false U.S. personas to organize and coordinate U.S. political rallies protesting the results of the 2016 U.S. presidential election. For example, in or around November 2016, they organized a rally in New York through one controlled group designed to "show your support for President-Elect Donald Trump" held on or about November 12, 2016. At the same time, through another controlled group, they organized a rally in New York called "Trump is NOT my President" held on or about November 12, 2016. Similarly, they organized a rally titled "Charlotte Against Trump" in Charlotte, North Carolina, held on or about November 19, 2016.

https://www.justice.gov/file/1035477/download

FULL TEXT OF INDICTMENT 2-16-18

CHAPTER 29.

DO GHOSTWRITERS AND PROFESSIONAL COMMUNICATORS HAVE A RESPONSIBILITY AS MORAL AGENTS?

In public relations, most of us do a considerable amount of writing for other people. A ghostwriter, as such, writes speeches, statements, talking points officially credited to another person as the author. The ghostwriter steps into the character of a subject and produces communication that emulates the individual in tone, tenor, persona and style. A ghostwriter can greatly enhance the image of a subject.

However, there are personal decisions to make in how we, as ghostwriters, enhance the images of other people that raise the question, Do we have a responsibility as moral agents? A moral agent is said to be one who is capable of acting with reference to right and wrong.

For example, is it right or wrong to enhance the image of a subject beyond what is deserved of the person's intelligence, judgement and capabilities? How far beyond?

Is it right or wrong for us to correct or ignore a subject's unwitting tendency to overstep the boundaries of civility and respect?

Is it right or wrong for us to support, ignore or rationalize a subject's propensity to lie and deceive?

As ghostwriters, do we see ourselves as moral agents? If so, how do we account for our actions using the personal freedom we have to shape the persona of others resulting in praiseworthy or blameworthy human behavior?

Being a moral agent applies to professional communicators who disseminate information directly or through the media. Moral agents in high places of government, for example, can influence the mood, behavior and actions of entire nations. The U.S. White House press secretary is an example of such a moral agent, someone in a position to make moral judgments about disseminating truthful or untruthful information through the media to millions of people.

Consider the potential influence of U.S. press secretary Sarah Sanders when she appeared on "Fox News Sunday" Jan. 6, 2019, in an interview with Chris Wallace and falsely said that last year there were "nearly 4,000 known or suspected terrorists that CPB picked up that came across our southern border." Wallace interjected, saying he had "studied up" on the statistic. "Do you know where those 4,000 people come [from], where they're captured? Airports!" Wallace said.

Figures from the federal government's Department of Customs and Border Protection reveal that only six people on a security watchlist were detained over a six-month period. The grossly inflated figure has been regarded widely as a deliberate effort by the administration to generate public fear of immigrants at the southern border and support for the declaration of a national emergency by President Donald Trump for building a border wall. This example illustrates the responsibility professional communicators have as moral agents in deciding what is right and what is wrong.

CHAPTER 30.

CRISIS COMMUNICATION: A READINESS REVIEW

A crisis is not the time to be arguing about whether to behave for the court of law or the court of public opinion, as though they are mutually exclusive.

This review of your crisis communication readiness can be helpful in two ways. One, obviously, is to provide a quick check to see that essential actions are covered. But more importantly, it facilitates what I call the Rule of Advanced Engagement. It enables all individuals who are likely to be engaged in managing a crisis to see how people fit into the operation and discuss in advance with others how they plan to work together. They can also talk about principles they will maintain. A crisis is not the time to be arguing, for example, about whether to behave for the court of law or the court of public opinion, as though they are mutually exclusive.

General practice is for "crisis communication" responsibilities to be heaped on the person in charge of public relations. But the scope of work is so great that it takes a team of people to handle a situation. The person in charge must be free of logistical activities, like answering phone calls and worrying about the arrival of TV trucks, to work with executive managers in assessing a situation. To do that, the person in charge must be able to rely on others with various skills who are pre-selected and trained to assist. The person in charge must have a team and must be the leader of that team, always at the ready.

A situation team must be more than a gaggle of staffers organized on the fly. A good communication preparedness team includes individuals from different departments, such as human resources, IT and security. They are people trained and on call, like members of a volunteer fire department. The phrase, "We have a situation..." tells team members to drop what they are doing and assemble in a situation room that is totally set up and properly equipped with all necessary electronic devices in place and operational.

When a situation develops, a team leader (or alternate) should be able to walk into a situation room in which staff and other personnel are already in place and operating as follows:

- monitoring and recording news and social media;
- ready with a hotline open for incoming questions and gathering information;
- in place to log, record and schedule return phone calls;
- on hand to video record interviews with executives;
- standing by to take journalists to an assembly site, if instructed;
- ready to take media representatives on restricted tours, if directed;
- in place with the organization's special communication website page up and ready;
- on hand to ensure proper IT operation of all electronic equipment;
- in place watching over the human safety and physical security of the situation room.

This chapter divides crisis communication activities into sections so that 1) everyone can see and appreciate roles and responsibilities 2) principles of operation can be discussed in advance of a situation, and 3) senior management can see the substantial number of human and physical resources necessary for an effective communication preparedness strategy.

We begin with the Situation Team.

SITUATION TEAM   Role and Responsibilities

A situation team is always "at the ready" to spring into action. The phrase, "We have a situation," triggers the organization's preparedness strategy and calls the situation team to assemble. The neutral word "situation" is used because whatever name is used initially will be the name used by everyone else going forward. Using the word "crisis," for example, could incorrectly prejudge something to be a crisis when, in fact, it could be something else. Following are roles and responsibilities of a situation team.

1. Handles basic communication activities and frees time for the Situation Team Leader to work closely with management

2. Monitors and records events and conditions as they develop

3. Assesses the situation treating perceived the same as actual conditions

4. Handles controlled media tours

5. Meets and greets media representatives and guides them to assembly areas

6. Provides media representatives with "house rules" with respect to proprietary matters

7. Ensures timely communication and sharing of information with all stakeholder groups

8. Communicates directly with appropriate bloggers,

if necessary

9. Seeks third party validations of the organization's claims and actions to protect its credibility

10. Seeks the truth of what happened

11. Ensures consistent messaging

12. Considers needs of everyone involved—employees, families, neighbors

13. Keeps policies current on the release of information, (e.g. names of victims, conditions, etc.)

14. Keeps policies current for handling inquiries from all sources

15. Keeps biographical data current on executive managers

16. Verifies information for accuracy

17. Works to speed public visibility of executive control, facts, updates

18. Makes correct use of tools—statements, bulletins, news briefings, press conferences,

19. Knows that reporters want prompt cooperation and a front seat to all action and information

20. Respects media's insistence for honesty, transparency, accuracy, timely actions, regular updates, equal access to information from knowledgeable sources, calls promptly returned

21. Knows that the name given to a situation is what it will be called by everyone else going forward

22. Uses World Wide Web to monitor mainstream

and social media references to a situation

23. Operates organization's Website page for special communication

24. Immediately corrects erroneous news reports

25. Immediately spikes rumors

26. Looks for opportunities to recognize praiseworthy behaviors of first responders and others

27. Knows the difference between handling crisis and risk communication—crisis being something that has happened; risk being something yet to happen

28. Knows to communicate risk—when risk is immediate; under investigation; likely to be revealed; likely to be explained by others; when based on questionable data; on fairly dependable data; when suspected; even when it doesn't yet make sense

29. Addresses risk to set the pace for resolution; allow meaningful public involvement; facilitates better control of information; leads on the offensive; earns public trust; averts a situation elsewhere

30. Knows risk communication should NOT be delayed because:

    1. people have a right to know immediately about any risk to their health and safety;

    2. because rumors begin;

    3. a situation becomes exaggerated;

    4. sense of anxiety elevates and turns to fear;

5. news breaks;

6. story is told from viewpoints of others;

7. cover-up is suspected;

8. trust plummets;

9. put on the defensive;

10. concern turns to resentment, to anger, to outrage

31. Cooperates with media.

32. Provides NO information about: dollar estimates of damage; estimates of insurance coverage or other settlements; names of injured or their condition; original cost estimates of equipment involved; number of persons injured, where taken for treatment; possible causes of the accident or incident; time estimates for resuming operation; what equipment was damaged; what happened; what is not known about the situation

33. Is accountable for every action, transparent as possible, clear on any government or non-profit money being spent in the response to an emergency

34. Seeks opportunities to go beyond event-specific information with data that provides greater context, understanding and accuracy of a situation

35. Prepares a final debriefing on a situation with follow-up actions

1. Manages the overall operation of the situation team

2. Confers continuously with executive management to assess a developing situation

3. Collects and evaluates data from situation team

4. Ensures that news media needs are met

5. Considers the needs of all stakeholder groups

6. Addresses the public's need to see management promptly—in view, in control, with details

7. Controls the rate of public response to reflect judgement, engagement, management

8. Thinks above a situation about perceptions, concentrations of interest, predispositions

9. Prepares executives for interviews

10. Conducts interview practice with executives to stay on message, use redundancies, emphasize that it is strong, not weak, to show emotion and human understanding

11. Focuses on what's on people's minds rather than what one thinks or should be on their minds

12. Practices direct communication—if necessary, calls or meets with bloggers, tweeters, or people behind Facebook, WhatsApp, WeChat, QZone, Tumblr, Instagram, Google+ and other social media.

13. Always professional—a major announcement is

not a progress report; a news briefing is not a press conference; a progress report is not a news release

14. Strives to be a moral agent, distinguishing between what's right and wrong

15. Communicates frequently on a scheduled basis even when there is little new to report

16. Decides with management whether or not to have executive interviews

17. Tunes in to community issues that might be of greater concern than an incident

18. Thinks of everything people want to know to determine community needs

19. Tries to meet the information needs of every interested group

EXECUTIVE *Role and Responsibilities*

1. Has interviews monitored by staff member and, if necessary, recorded

2. Does not go "off the record" for any reason

3. Appears promptly, in charge and taking action; does not wait for all the details to speak

4. Owns up to responsibilities

5. Tells the good and bad knowing people can cope with the truth

6. In speaking before television cameras, looks into the lens of the camera, like speaking to friends and neighbors

7. Is always aware that cameras and open mics can be anywhere, including restrooms, hallways, lobbies, parking lots, vendor carts, fast food stores

8. Provides details up-front, fast and as complete as possible

9. Addresses emotion first, then facts

10. Expresses genuine empathy in the first 30 seconds of starting a message, showing concern for people who may be feeling frightened, anxious, confused, wanting to know if "you get it."

11. Does not parcel out the truth

12. Is contrite, as appropriate

13. Reports the bad news, rather than having it told by others

14. Reassures that action steps are in progress, validated, if possible, by an independent third party

15. Tells what is known and lets people reach their own conclusions

16. Answers in short, simple sentences without volunteering details, explanations

17. Declines comment on speculation or comments by unidentified sources

18. Uses message points to stay in control of an interview

19. Graciously acknowledges and welcomes help

20. Expresses compassion for people's feelings

21. Treats every question with respect

22. Reflects honesty and openness while facing the realities of the situation

23. Addresses the public with the persona of a statesman or stateswoman showing a sense of integrity and impartial concern for the public good

24. Does what's right (e.g. "I'm told that we have no legal responsibility, but we're going to act as though we do."

25. Refutes anything that is disagreeable or inaccurate

26. Spikes rumors, corrects misinformation

27. Engages the public in the process and allows others to follow

28. Communicates with a natural confidence in an organization's state of preparedness

29. Treats journalists with respect for the job they are expected to do

30. Points out independent, third-party oversight of a situation

31. Treats a repeat question with same respect shown toward the original one

32. Acknowledges opposing views, then states or restates organization's position

33. When a situation is potentially adversarial, completely resists becoming tightly coiled, belligerent, combative, arrogant or defiant

34. Uses a conciliatory tone to engage listeners

35. Never utters the words, "There's no reason to be

afraid;" tells what is known to help others feel less afraid. "I understand that anything related to radiation can seem frightening. Let me tell you what I know…"

36. Is comfortable with taking long pauses and as much time that is needed

37. Shows concern for every question asked, and lets reporters know that answers will be forthcoming

38. Rephrases hostile questions to facilitate constructive answers. For example, a reporter might say: "How many other near-death mishaps have you had at this plant?" Restated in a positive way: "Are you asking what our safety record has been?

39. Knows that it is OK to act human and show emotion

40. Knows that refusing an interview gives others a chance to tell the story, often incorrectly

41. Knows that expressing a conclusion does not necessarily persuade others to accept it

42. Knows people have a right to know everything about risk that threatens their health and safety

43. Knows that telling half-truths erodes credibility

44. Knows that bridging to something related to a situation is better than bridging to an entirely different subject

45. Knows that people won't listen until empathy is expressed

46. Knows that action steps, more than words, reduce

anxiety and fear and help recovery

47. Knows to end interview before the questions begin to lose relevancy

TEAM LEADER AS SPOKESPERSON   *Role and Responsibilities*

1. Tells it first, fast, accurately

2. Addresses emotion first, then facts

3. Communicates before someone else does

4. Promises to tell the truth and never lie

5. Spikes rumors quickly with accurate data

6. Never goes off the record with the news media—no exceptions

7. Points out independent, third-party oversight of a situation

8. Puts risk into perspective using more than numbers

9. Knows that when it comes to personal risks, people want to hear from trusted sources with credible information

10. Treats people like intelligent adults

11. Avoids fueling a community's tendency to see risks as "safe" or "dangerous"

12. Stays engaged as long as necessary to answer every question

13. Tells what can be expected next and when more information will be available

14. Knows people have a right to know promptly

everything about risk that threatens their health and safety

15. Acknowledges opposing views, then states or restates organization's position

16. Corrects inaccurate information, spikes rumors

17. Is honest and forthright, but does not feel compelled to give away the store.

18. Talks to be understood and avoids the use of industry jargon

19. Schedules regular media briefings even when there may not be anything new to report

20. Knows that every word, eye twitch and passing emotion will be observed and often reported

21. Thinks of all possible questions, including the toughest ones and rehearses answers

22. Always comments; never says, "no comment"

23. Always aware that cameras and open mics can be anywhere, including restrooms, hallways, lobbies, parking lots, vendor carts, fast food stores

24. Prepares to calm nerves, not just explain the situation.

25. Useful phrases:

    1. We're following an investigative process and will provide details at the appropriate time... There is proprietary information involved that we cannot divulge...

    2. There are legal issues involved...

3. We've just learned of the situation and are getting information now…

4. I'm not an authority on the subject; I will put you in touch with…

5. We're preparing a statement and will have a copy for you…

6. We don't respond to comments from "unidentified sources"

7. We don't respond to rumors

8. Reassures that action steps are in progress

MANAGEMENT   *Role and Responsibilities*

1. Ranks preparedness on a par with all of the organization's operations

2. Orients all members on the organization's communication preparedness strategy

3. Explains the nature of incidents that trigger the preparedness strategy

4. Emphasizes that in any incident, the rule is to take care of people first

5. Knows members have a right to know promptly of any risk to their health and safety

6. Guides members in their role with the news media

7. Describes how members are valued as ambassadors of the organization

8. Explains how members can help obtain and dis-

seminate information

9. Engages members to be participants, rather than spectators in a preparedness strategy

10. Instills in members a natural confidence that all together, "We're prepared."

11. Provides the human and physical resources to support a communication preparedness capability, annually.

CHAPTER 31.

IMPROVE YOUR PUBLIC RELATIONS WRITING IN 16 CONTROLLABLE WAYS

How often have you said to yourself, "This time what I write is going to be really good!" How often have you felt disappointed that you are not making much progress in your writing? You know, practice doesn't necessarily make perfect. Practice, alone, can simply re-enforce habits that keep your writing from improving. You can change that by knowing elements that you can control to make your writing highly effective. Here are 16 writing elements you can control to sharpen your writing skills.

Know that a public relations writer has the opportunity to set the standard for communication throughout an organization. Look around you and notice how others are communicating—educators, doctors, engineers, etc. But don't try to imitate the way they write. Instead, be an effective writer and set the standard for them.

There are four elements you can control in **preparing a message**: 1) Be clear—write in plain talk, use details people can visualize. 2) Be brief—write in simple, declarative statements. 3) Be direct—use active verbs and comfortable words. 4) Yes, by all means, be human—write as a personal conversation. If any of these elements seem contrary to the way people in your organization write, be courageous. Win them over to writing to a new standard.

Let's look at four more controllable elements that will enable you to **connect with people**. These four elements should be included in the opening of whatever you are writing. Provide the big picture—the broad context for your communication. Answer the question: "What's this about?" Provide the purpose of your communication—why you are communicating (e.g. to inform, alert, announce, etc.) Answer the question: "Why should I care?" Pique people's interest. Answer the question: "What's in it for me?" Finally, provide the thesis of your communication. Answer the question: "What's your point?"

Now you are getting something specific to practice. Challenge yourself to answer those four questions in the opening of communication on any media platform.

So far, I've covered preparing the message and connecting with people. Next let's look at what you must do to **maintain the connection** with receivers of your message. First is persona—the level of expertise you must bring to the subject. Second is tone—the attitude you convey toward the subject. Third is voice—the personality you project. Fourth is style—the distinct or characteristic way you have the message delivered (e.g. length of sentences)

The next four controllable elements are meant to cause people to think about your communication long enough to **influence their behavior**. Convey your message through a story—something motivating, inspirational, a situation that makes them wonder what they would do—a call to action. Or make an emotional plea—tug at what they care about. Or surprise them—seek action through something people haven't thought about. Or fill your message with validity—lots of details, convincing data, third party endorsements. Practice can make perfect now that you know what to practice.

SIXTEEN CONTROLLABLE WAYS TO IMPROVE YOUR WRITING

Preparing Messages

CLEAR—plain talk, using details receivers can visualize

BRIEF—simple, declarative statements

DIRECT—active verbs and comfortable words

HUMAN—like a personal conversation

Connecting with Receivers

PICTURE—the broad context of your communication

PURPOSE—why you are communicating to inform, alert, announce…

PIQUE—what's in it for the receivers–pique interest

POINT—your main point—thesis

Maintaining the Connection with Receivers

PERSONA—level of expertise you must bring to the subject

TONE—attitude you convey toward the subject

VOICE—personality you project

STYLE—distinct or characteristic way the message is delivered

Making Messages Last Long Enough to Influence Behavior

EMOTIONAL—tug at what they care about

STORY—motivating, inspirational, what they would do, call to action

SURPRISE—seek action, something people haven't thought about

VALIDITY—lots of details, convincing data, third party endorsements

CHAPTER 32.

GOING OFF THE RECORD? DON'T GET STUNG!

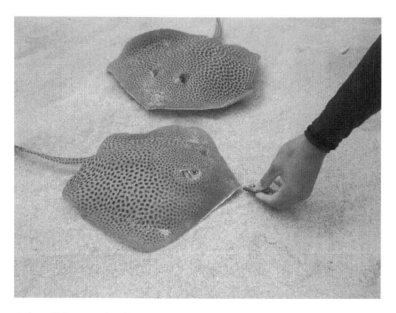

Going off the record with reporters is like feeding stingrays and hoping not to experience the pain of an unexpected barb that may not be life-threatening, but gravely threatening in other ways.

This chapter clarifies the meanings of "off the record," "on background," and "on deep background," and should be of interest to anyone who has occasion to speak to reporters.

When I heard the news about a White House staff member, Madeleine Westerhout, resigning over the issue of going off the record with reporters about the President's family, I thought immediately of my grandson Ben, at age three, performing with a mic and amplifier his original song, wailing endlessly, "Why, oh why? Why, oh why? Why, oh why…."

To respond to my grandson's question, for our purposes, I would say, "Why would you want to risk even one night's sleep worrying about whether or not what you told a reporter off the record will, in fact, be kept off the record and not featured with you as the source in tomorrow's headlines?" I never had even one sleepless night over this trust issue because I never went off the record, and doing so never adversely affected my career in any way.

In my view, going off the record with reporters is like feeding stingrays and hoping not to experience the pain of an unexpected barb that may not be life-threatening, but gravely threatening in other ways. For White House aide, Madeleine Westerhout, going off the record about the President's family apparently was considered an act of disloyalty and cost her a job. Consider what was at stake for this young woman.

Westerhout, 28, served as special assistant to the president and when she resigned was director of Oval Office

Operations. She was one of the highest-paid White House staffers with a salary of $145,000. The California native moved to the East Coast to attend the College of Charleston as a political science major. She took the fall semester of her senior year off to intern for Mitt Romney's 2012 presidential campaign. She worked on Capitol Hill after graduation, and then served as assistant to a former Republican National Committee chief of staff. She reportedly incurred great, tearful pain by going off the record.

This story should heighten your interest in how you interact with reporters, but not shake your confidence in working effectively with the press. When reporters show up, some managers have been known to sneak out the back door. There's no need to feel that way when you know the basics about communicating "on the record," "off the record," "on background," and "on deep background."

When talking with a reporter, everything is "on the record." All that you say can be quoted directly or indirectly and attributed to your name for the public to see. If you think before you speak, you can converse cooperatively and confidently with a reporter for any length of time without giving him or her anything inflammatory to write about. Consider what I call "protective phrases," to be used earnestly, honestly and politely in all forms of media:

"Are you trying to put words in my mouth?"

"Would you rephrase that question without the implications?"

"I didn't say that."

"I'd like to help you with that, but you know what must be done first."

"You know why I can't provide that, at least not at this time."

"Why would you ask it that way?"

"You know why we have to follow a process."

"Those are your words, not mine."

"We make it a practice not to respond to speculation or rumor."

"Is there something specific you want to know?"

You will want to rely on protective phrases, such as these, when you learn the complexities of "going off the record."

What does "off the record" mean to reporters? To some, it means that off the record information can't be attributed to its source. To some, it means that the information can't be attributed to its source and can't be used. To some, it means that the information can be used and attributed to some broadly identifying sources, such as a staff, a team, member of an organization, but not to a specifically named individual. To some, it means that while off the record information can't be used in a news story, it can be talked about it to friends, family and co-workers.

To some, it means nothing, knowing that the information can be obtained from and attributed to other sources. Off the record has no legal standing. There are no laws to break. No rules of accountability. It's a trust issue. There's no taking back what you said, or retroactively making what you said, "off the record." You can see how easily this phrase can be misunderstood by a news source and reporter. That's why it is best never to go off the record—without exception.

When you speak to a reporter "on background," it means to most journalists that they may use the information, but in no way or fashion, identify, quote or hint about the source. Another way to say that is the information you provide is "not for attribution." True, this can mean a lot to a journalist who is trying to learn about something that is otherwise new, unknown, or not understood by him or her. Granted, a reporter will be forever grateful for your help in developing a story. But the same cautions apply that dangle on a trust relationship for going off the record with a reporter.

"On deep background" means a journalist can report the information, but cannot cite where it came from. Cannot, should not—once again, a trust issue. Think of how critical the matter of trust is to a whistleblower!

Never assume that you and a reporter are agreeing to the same terms. Always spell out the ground rules. Mutually agree to them in advance. Think twice about who stands to gain the most from divulging information—you, a reporter, the general public. Think about the consequences to yourself if the trust breaks down in going off the record, on background, on deep background.

CHAPTER 33.

A SECRET TO PERSUASIVE WRITING

Art of Persuasion: Write for Results

A secret to persuasive writing is to clear away obstacles, then write for results. I can't tell you how to write persuasively until you have something to write about. That's because the art of persuasion is about more than writing;

it's about clearing away obstacles to persuasion, then writing for results. To illustrate what I mean, consider this persuasive writing assignment:

Write remarks for a public meeting to persuade community residents to accept the siting of a methadone treatment facility in their neighborhood.

What do you see as obstacles in the way of persuading community residents to accept the siting of a methadone treatment facility in their neighborhood? You know that methadone is a synthetic opioid used in the treatment of people addicted to heroin. So you could surmise that residents could easily fear that such a facility will attract drug users and dealers. You could surmise that residents could be quick to protest with cries of NIMBYism, "Not in my backyard!" The point is, it will be difficult, if not impossible, to reason with people that a treatment facility is a non-threatening, worthwhile service to the community until the obstacles of ignorance and fear are cleared away.

Keep in mind that to persuade is not the same as to convince. There's a difference. It's important to know that persuading is reasoning with someone to get them to do something. Convincing is using facts and evidence to make a case, but stops short of persuading, in that no action is expected. So we are interested in persuasion—reasoning with someone to get them to do what you want. It's a matter of getting them to take an action that will give you the behavior you want.

Persuasion requires more than staring into space, wondering what words to use. Persuasion requires more than applying certain writing techniques. Persuasion requires more than producing communication free of errors in spelling, grammar, punctuation and style. Persuasion relies heavily on your ability to analyze, identify obstacles standing in the way of persuasion, to develop solutions for removing obstacles, and finally to write for results.This problem-solving ability comes from personal experiences you have had, and all that you have learned, formally and informally, in the liberal arts areas of psychology, sociology, geography, history, philosophy, ethics, languages and the sciences. Give yourself credit for the wonderful ability you have acquired that should be featured in resumes and discussed in job interviews. Think about it... Your background in liberal arts contributes to the way you think, the way you read critically, the ways you collect and organize facts and form ideas. Liberal arts, or whatever you'd like to call it, is the basis for the art of persuasion and writing for results.

Apply what I just told you to this persuasive writing assignment:

Dissuade commissioners from showcasing steel in the architectural design of an airport expansion.

There is little anyone can put into words, alone, that would get the desired result of getting commissioners to consider a broader choice of materials with which to design an airport expansion. Trying, in words, to dissuade commissioners from favoring the use of one material in the design of the airport expansion is the obstacle to persuasion in this assignment. There is a lot that can be put into images to show that some of the most impressive architectural designs for airport expansions are in combinations of aluminum, glass and steel. Such recognition could clear away the obstacle of not being able to make a case with words alone. Perhaps sending a photographer to a half dozen airports to get architectural award-deserving images of expansions done in multiple materials and combining those images with a written script would accomplish the assignment. This was an actual case successfully accomplished. Clear the obstacles, then write for results.

What about this assignment?

Dissuade six nations from responding to a trade crisis with punitive measures.

The U.S. Trade Representative issued a public request for solutions to a trade crisis. A cash-starved nation is dumping a commodity on world markets, driving prices below the cost of production in six nations. Would you, as public relations vice president of a firm affected by the crisis, have the knowledge on hand to offer as a solution to the crisis. Probably not, at least not at the ready. Therein is the obstacle. But suppose that in working with others in your organization, you come up with a possible solution, like self-imposed production limits by individual nations, working within anti-trust laws, to distribute the oversupply of the commodity at issue over a manageable period of time, thus avoiding any need for adversarial trade measures. You have cleared away the obstacle and now you can write a persuasive case for your solution's application. This was an actual case. The solution was selected by the U.S. Trade Representative and used as the base document for solving a potential trade crisis among six nations. Clear the obstacles, write for results.

Let's consider one final persuasive writing assignment:

Write copy for a persuasive brochure that will generate, in no more than two weeks, $250,000 in donations to pay initial costs of hosting an international exhibit of Japanese art.

Do you have a magical combination of words with which to accomplish this assignment? An obvious obstacle is the time factor of raising a great amount of money in a very short time. Another obstacle is trying to achieve the desired result with traditionally slow fundraising tactics. Perhaps it was something in the writer's experience or background in the arts and in business that said forget asking for donations and instead provide irresistible funding opportunities. The idea caught on among fundraising committee members and a brochure draft of irresistible funding opportunities sold out completely for $250,000 in two weeks—even before it could be printed! Actual case. Clear the obstacles to persuasion, then write for results.

From these examples of actual cases, you can see that persuasion requires more than applying writing techniques. Persuasive writing relies heavily on your ability to analyze a situation, identify and deal with obstacles standing in the way of persuasion. You can see how this ability includes personal experiences you have had and all that you have learned, formally and informally, in the areas of psychology, sociology, geography, history, philosophy, ethics, languages, and the sciences. These areas of liberal arts contribute to the way you think, read critically, collect and organize facts, and form ideas. They form the basis for persuasive writing.

CHAPTER 34.

DOES YOUR USE OF ENGLISH GRAMMAR REFLECT THE IMAGE OF A PROFESSIONAL?

In many cases, all it takes is one grammatical error, spoken or written, to cast into question the professional ability of a reporter, broadcast journalist or public relations specialist. This chapter presents an opportunity for you to determine whether or not it is time for you to refresh your knowledge of English grammar. Following is a mixed list of correct and incorrect applications of English grammar. Make a list of correct applications and check your choices with the list of correct applications at the end of this chapter.

1. The city council, including staff members, was asked to attend.

2. He and I like the way things are being handled.

3. As for the American public, their views on gun control are highly nuanced.

4. A majority of Americans wants stricter gun laws.

5. There are a number of places that we could visit.

6. A list of infractions are being reviewed.

7. None is in favor of building the bridge.

8. A bouquet of roses beautify the space.

9. Neither Martin nor Joan is available.

10. The clock should stay just where it's at.

11. There's a lot of people here today.

12. The majority of voters rejects the proposed oil terminal.

13. The staff is deciding how they want to vote.

14. If Abby were in charge, we wouldn't be concerned about this.

15. I wish it were on another day.

16. It is he.

17. He spoke quicker than she did.

18. It is I who am at fault.

19. It's you who's not telling the truth.

20. Each of the girls reads the journal.

21. Wendy is as angry as her.

22. Dick is more qualified than me.

23. The men each gave their support.

24. Alan asked my mother and I.

25. Her and her friend told us about it.

26. I called he and Georgia.

27. Who gave permission?

28. Whom should I give this to?

29. A person whom I think should be congratulated is here.

30. George is the one that called it to our attention.

31. He is on the squad that saved the children.

32. The note, which was also collected, did not provide a clue.

33. Where did you get this at?

34. Cleveland, along with five other Northern cities, has asked for more federal aid.

35. A better training course for firefighters and a new fire station is high on his list of goals for his administration.

36. I am anxious to meet him.

37. George deserves the compliment.

38. The team is comprised of experts who are trained in cyber warfare.

39. The restaurant is 10 miles further on the right.

40. A majority of the houses were destroyed

41. The majority has decided not to announce its decision.

42. A number of accidents are expected.

43. The number of people is less than expected.

44. Between you and I, this is not the way to do it.

45. Our instructor has asked Peter and I to work together on the problem.

46. We use to do it that way.

47. Students that live off campus need to be contacted.

48. He took a turn for the worse.

49. The boss cancelled the meeting since we need more time to catch up.

50. The player was laying on the field with help on the way.

Remember, in many cases, all it takes is one grammatical error, spoken or written, to cast into question your professional ability. It is never too late to refresh your knowledge of English grammar.

CORRECT APPLICATIONS OF ENGLISH GRAMMAR

1, 2, 3, 7, 9, 12, 13, 14, 15, 16, 18, 20, 23, 27, 28, 31, 32, 34, 37, 41, 42, 43, 48

CHAPTER 35.

EASILY OVERCOME WRITER'S BLOCK

To easily clear away writer's block, we need to refresh our view. In many cases, we create a block because we focus too much on ourselves, rather than on the receivers of our communication.

Receivers today suffer from information overload. Your communication can be regarded as an annoying interruption. "What's this about?" they ask. Tell them upfront, in a sentence or two. Give them the big picture, broadly, but succinctly.

"Why should I care?" they ask. Tell them the purpose of your communication.

"What's in it for me?" they persist. Pique their interest. Tell them how your communication is of benefit to them and hold their attention long enough to make your point.

Focus on the receivers of your communication. Cover the 4Ps in an order that fits the application.

- Give them the big *picture*.
- Tell them your *purpose*.
- *Pique* their interest.
- Make your *point*.
- Writer's block goes away when you concentrate on delivering the 4Ps. The application is virtually universal to everything you write. Let's look at some examples.

EXAMPLE OF USING THE 4P FORMULA

[Picture] We have a growing number of employees whose work spans so many time zones that 18-hour workdays are routine. Our globetrotting managers are remarkable for their unswerving emotional presence with people they work with–even when our employees, say, in China, call during dinner.

[Purpose] We know this is not a healthy situation for employees. Long hours pose the risk of burnout and lost creativity, and ripple out to touch all facets of employees' lives. We want to do more to protect your health.

[Pique Interest] With your help, we can find alternative ways to reduce long hours. Conventional approaches to flexibility, such as flextime, don't help our "time-zone warriors" because waves of transoceanic calls wipe out workday boundaries. This is your opportunity to reduce workday hours.

[Point] When someone calls from China, it's OK to say, I'm feeding the kids; can we set another time to talk?" Global demands are speeding workplace cultures toward greater trust, a tighter focus on goals and more openness about personal conflicts. With your participation we hope to find alternative time-management solutions. Let us know your thoughts. Write directly to me.

SAMPLE APPLICATIONS OF THE 4P FORMULA

- Memo
- Backgrounder
- Issue Bulletin
- Letter
- Biographical Sketch
- Media Alert

MEMO

[context] You probably noticed that we have had an increasing number of visitors lately. That's mostly because of our new contract with the government.

[pique interest] Federal officials have been coming to see the facility and some have been bringing cameras and asking to take pictures in your production area.

[purpose] The purpose of this memo is to remind everyone about our policy governing photography.

[main point] In the production area we have customized, proprietary equipment which, for competitive reasons, must be kept secret.

[segue to body text] Following is a restatement of our company policy on photography and imaging devices.

BACKGROUNDER

[context] There is widespread confusion in the public mind about the synthetically produced drug methadone. There is also widespread confusion among doctors about the drug and its use.

[pique interest] Everyone who has an interest in methadone should be clear on its use.

[purpose] The purpose of this paper is to provide background on the composition, application and consequences of using methadone.

[main point] Methadone is effective in the treatment of drug addiction and for the relief of pain.

[segue to body text] Following is information that will clear up confusion about the drug methadone.

ISSUE BULLETIN

[context] Several members of the Washington State Legislature have introduced a measure that would rescind tax credits previously granted to companies as an incentive to locate operations in the state.

[pique interest] Such a measure, if passed into law, would reflect negatively on the state's integrity causing prospective businesses to reconsider locating in the state and causing existing recipients of tax credits to reconsider long-range expansion plans in the state.

[purpose] The purpose of this bulletin is to issue a call to action by businesses throughout the state notifying them to contact elected state officials and urge them not to consider proposed H.B. 2023 eliminating tax credits.

[main point] Action against this measure is needed immediately.

LETTER

Dear Mr. Horner:

[context] The city has no land available in your part of the city for public recreation.

[pique interest] There are 1100 children, ages 4 to 12, living within a two-mile radius of your business. These children and their families need a safe area in which to socialize and play.

[purpose] The purpose of this letter is to ask you to

donate to the city a part of your property for a public park that could be named "Horner's Corner."

[main point] We have organized a neighborhood committee that would like to meet with you soon to discuss this idea in more detail.

[segue to body] Following is a general description of our proposal.

BIOGRAPHICAL SKETCH

[context] This is a biographical sketch of April Ellemay Hutchinson. She was founder and owner of Hutchinson Cybergraphics, Inc.

[purpose] The purpose of this sketch is to outline her career.

[pique interest] Artists are particularly interested in her unique design concepts and sources of inspiration.

[main point] April Hutchinson is held in high esteem by advertising brand managers throughout the world.

[segue to body text] Hutchinson's career began in a studio loft of a barn in Delonahga, Georgia.

MEDIA

[context] This is National Preparedness Month.

[pique interest] Local emergency services units have been urging people to prepare for a bird flu pandemic.

[purpose] The purpose of this advisory is to call attention

to an exhibit that will be on display at the Arc Exhibition Center provided by the Federal Emergency Management Agency.

[main point] Mayor George Byrd will announce and describe the city's emergency plan at the opening of the exhibit.

[Next — the what, when, where, details.]

You just received the 4P formula for meeting the challenges of communicating effectively with your receivers. No writer's block. The path is clear for you to carry on.

CHAPTER 36.

NAVIGATING OVER ROCKS OF DISTRUST

BUILDING TRUST

This seems to be the right time to be talking about trust. In every area of activity today people are struggling to navigate rivers of distrust. Leaders of some organizations are asking, How low can it go?" They are reaching out for help when, in fact, qualified help is on their payroll.

Newsletter editors are already stepping into larger roles. They are using many different forms of electronic communication to reach employees and all stakeholder groups. They are on-board, knowledgeable communicators perfectly capable of helping to create, build and restore cultures of trust. After all, who is closer to the "voice of the people?" Who in management has a better understanding of what trust means to employees? Who is better able to see the erosion or growth of trust in an organization?

To unleash the potential of its "trust builders," organizations should take actions to show that newsletter editors are employed not to act as the voice of management, but rather to liaise with employees on all levels toward the goal of operating within a culture of trust. Newsletter editors on every communication platform should be ready to step up to this new responsibility as the footings of organizations and institutions get pounded by bigger and bigger rocks of distrust and strain to navigate shallow waters.

Specifically, how can newsletter editors help create cultures of trust?

"The Neuroscience of Trust," article by Paul J. Zak in the Jan-Feb 2017 issue of Harvard Business Review identified management actions that build trust. Think about the kinds of articles newsletter editors could write in each of the following areas that help build trust: 1. employee recognition; 2. progress being made toward achievable goals; 3. employees empowered to figure things out; 4. employees enabled to focus on what they care about; 5.

open, daily communication about company activities and direction; 6. employees encouraged to express interest in and concern for others; 7. management interest in job performance, but also in personal growth; 8. management allowing that it's ok for supervisors and managers to ask employees for help. The author's overall conclusion was cultivate trust by setting a clear direction, giving people what they need to see it through and getting out of their way.

CHAPTER 37.

FIVE TIPS BEYOND THE BASICS OF SPEECHWRITING

There are many good sources for instruction in public speaking. I cannot say enough about the expert instruction I was fortunate to get from Anett Grant, founder and CEO of Executive Speaking, Inc. Anett has been coaching leaders and emerging leaders for the past 37 years. She was gracious enough to give me permission to share some of her basic techniques with students. What follows, however, is what I have learned on my own through personal observation and experience in ghostwriting for executives. Consider what follows as small tips with big impacts that go hand-in-hand with executive coaching.

TIP #1   Look straight ahead, sometimes, and speak to the whole audience

It is common for speakers to use teleprompters. When you watch speakers on TV, you will see them reading, first from a teleprompter stand on the left, then from one on the right. "Presidential Teleprompters," so called because they are used by U.S. presidents, are transparent glass panels that look like music stands and are positioned on either side of a podium to make it seem like the speaker has eye contact with an entire audience. However, some speakers do a constant back and forth head swivel and even include a body shift of their weight from one leg to another, a distracting, conspicuous, unprofessional use of teleprompters. But even more important, by looking only side to side a speaker can seem to be ignoring the largest part of, say, a TV audience of thousands or millions of viewers by never looking straight at them into the camera. This makes TV viewers, for example, feel like "on-lookers" to an event. It also makes it impossible to emphasize main points to those feeling like on-lookers. With practice, a speaker can use the assistance of teleprompting equipment in a more natural way that makes all viewers feel that they are being personally addressed by the speaker.

A word of advice to the public relations practitioner who hires teleprompting services for a big presidential type setup or a basic on-camera event. In both cases, you are a customer paying for a service. You are responsible to a client for the successful use of a  service. That means you have to be in charge of the service, getting what you know your client wants. You cannot meet this responsibility by abrogating it to a service provider who boasts about knowing what's best based on years of experience, technical competencies and successful events. Listen to recommendations, but rely on your own intuition, judgement and knowledge of your client. In practical terms, think of yourself bringing a script, most likely written by you, asking to have it loaded on the equipment by a teleprompter operator *that you expect to get with the equipment on the day of the event.* Review and edit the script with the operator to adjust the length of lines, maintain short sentence paragraphs, add marks for emphasis or pronunciation. Then rehearse the script standing in for your client, testing the teleprompter operator's attention to speeding up, slowing down, pausing, generally staying in synch with the speaker. If the service seems to have a problem with taking direction from you, find another service.

The advice provided above for hiring teleprompting services applies to services for graphic design, writing, photography, etc. To illustrate: Is it ok for you to look through the photographer's camera lens when a shot is set up? Of course it's ok! You're the customer. You're paying for the service. It is likely that the requirements you have are for someone other than yourself, such as a client or employer. So you cannot afford to cave in to service providers who insist on doing the job "their way," based on their years of experience, extensive training, and professional knowledge.

One way to deal with hiring and directing professional

services is to discuss the assignment, listen to suggestions, make up your own mind and insist first on doing the job according to your requirements, then if time permits, doing it "their way" to present possible options. Keep in mind that you will be billed for all "options" requiring extra time. Trust your own thinking, regardless of the limited or broader extent of your experience or training. Otherwise you likely will find yourself back at square one doing the job you were told to do in the first place.

TIP #2   About eyeglasses.

Many speakers take for granted the use of eye glasses. They do not think about the image they project, for example, when they peer over glasses with bifocal lenses perched on the tips of their noses. Some think that makes them look intelligent, authoritative,  knowledgeable, wise. Others think that makes them look intimidating, arrogant, condescending, unapproachable. One suggestion is to eliminate the need for bifocal glasses by increasing the font size of type to be used in a speaker's script.

Take a look at these photos of former presidential candidate Jeb Bush with and without eyeglasses. How would you assess his campaign image? Add this to your assessment: Harvard Business School professor Amy Cuddy, in her new book, "Presence," says people quickly answer two questions when they first meet you: Can I trust this person? Can I respect this person? Psychologists refer to these dimensions as warmth and competence respectively, and ideally you want to be perceived as having both.

TIP #3   *Keep audience noise top of mind.*

A good speechwriter keeps audience noise top of mind from beginning to end of a presentation. Audience noise, in this case, refers to distractions in the minds of individual audience members. Close your eyes for a moment. Picture your presenter before a large audience about to read what you have written. Are people on the edge of their seats, waiting eagerly to hear your presenter's message? Unless their lives are depending on it, it is more likely that they are sifting through random thoughts of various degrees of importance. For example: I wonder how long this is going to take? Was I supposed to pick up from daycare today? Have to fill up the gas tank on the way home. What was it we need to take to the cabin this weekend? Who does Charlie think he is, saying the merger doesn't make sense! Olive oil! That's what we need at the cabin!

A successful ghostwriter must never take audience noise for granted. It is an ever-present challenge, especially where there is a collection of human brains parked with the motor running. What breaks through audience noise is not the content of a speech, but how it is crafted and organized: What is the main message? How is it supported? Is repetition used, how, and to what extent? What is the role of redundancy? In what order is the content arranged? The point is that content, alone, cannot break through audience noise. The attention of a human mind can be captured and led though distracting noise with writing techniques that can make a memorable, even action-driven impression.

TIP #4 *Have your speaker be straight with the audience.*

No jokes. Don't waste hours on trying to be funny with a speaker's opening statement. Don't take chances on starting formal remarks with humor. Especially, don't make your speaker bomb with a joke because most likely it will be as funny to the audience as getting a flat tire and arriving late. Time is spent better on developing a message of great relevance to a particular audience. And by the way, in this age of electronics, a speaker would be well advised to remember that there could be voice and visual surveillance from the time the speaking venue is entered to beyond the time it is exited.

TIP #5   *Urge your speaker to notate naturally felt gestures in the speaker's script.*

Not everyone is a natural performer, but everyone can learn to use natural gestures in making a speech or giving a presentation. We will get to the gestures, but first we need something in which to insert them, like the hardcopy of a speech or presentation. Speaker's scripts take a variety of forms. Let's use one I followed throughout my career.

I put a slug in normal type in the upper left corner to identify the script. Then I turn on page numbering. If ever a script is dropped, the pages can be reordered quickly *if they are numbered*. I use a 20-point sans serif type bold, sentence length of three or four words, paragraphs no more than two sentences (so a speaker can look up, recall and deliver one paragraph at a time), margins left and right of two inches, paragraphs indented, spacing set to 1 1/2 to 2 lines, and two hits of the return key to paragraph.

Now we have a structure into which we can notate gestures. I found it best to ask the speaker to write in notations for gestures. I also advise a speaker to keep one's place with an index finger on the script. That avoids embarrassment in making, say, a sweeping gesture and having to look down and search for your next remark. Naturally felt gestures include hand motions, facial expressions, pauses, raised or lowered voice, foot stomping, fist pounding, and whatever else helps a speaker emphasize the message. Finally, I advise a speaker to slide pages from left to right on the podium to hide the distraction of page turning. Look into purchasing a speaker's box which is made specifically to conceal page turning.

CHAPTER 38.

WHAT YOU NEED TO KNOW IN WRITING FOR EXECUTIVES

Think of your subject's persona, tone, voice and style.

This chapter will help prepare you for that inevitable

call—to see a vice president, executive director or chief executive officer. It will help you keep your sense of independent thinking when you step into an executive's office to discuss an assignment. It's OK to be in awe of the extraordinary amounts of money paid to chief executives, but it's not correct to assume that extraordinary pay stands for extraordinary business competencies. Maintain your independent thinking. Judge for yourself. Executives aren't always right, nor do they have all the answers.

Your public relations training has equipped you with skills that are invaluable to executives . You are a writer. You are a professional communicator. You know the process and fundamentals of how to persuade people to support, to vote, to consider, to champion, to follow, to read, to buy, to trust, to invest, to listen, to join, to leave alone, to contribute, to believe, to work, to authorize, to accept, to welcome, to compromise, to accommodate, to cooperate, to wait, to decide and the list goes on and on. You know how to influence behavior through strategic communication.

Executives have no such training. That's why it's essential to think for yourself. Don't assume that the person at the top knows everything. Use your skills, knowledge and intuitive sense of public relations to challenge your subject. Ask questions: Is this what you mean, or would it be more understandable if we said... Are you directing this just to this audience? Do we want to include other stakeholder groups? This could be misinterpreted; could we put it this way?

As a writer, you have an opportunity to challenge, suggest, recommend, shape an image, project statesmanship, amplify leadership characteristics, inject leading edge managerial concepts from your reading of business news, periodicals and books, write quotes. These insights should be helpful to you in understanding your relationship with executives. Closely observe your subject. You want to be able to write in a manner that is close to the way your subject writes and speaks. Your observations and subsequent writing should take into account four areas:

1. One is persona. It should reflect your subject's level of expertise.

2. Another is tone—the attitude your subject has for a particular message.

3. Another is voice—your subject's personality.

4. And another is style—the distinct or characteristic way in which your subject communicates—e.g. rapid, short, phrases; complete sentences delivered thoughtfully, etc.

You will know you did a good job when your subject says, "That's just the way I would have written (or said) it." You will know it was even better than your subject could have done. Your subject will claim credit for your writing and ownership of everything you did to make the communication effective and... Yes, you have to write the song and let your subject sing it and take the bows. The reward is in getting to write more and more for your subject. And that's why you can expect to be called on more and more. You will get to know not only how he or she writes and speaks, but how the individual thinks. This will make you even more valuable because you can crystalize concepts, clarify messages, insert leading edge theories, project leadership , shape a strong executive image. This is so very possible for a writer to do, and overdo. What if, through the power of your pen, the image you create begins to significantly exceed your subject's competencies? What can you do to protect your integrity as a writer, as well as the integrity of your subject? That's a matter for case by case consideration. It does happen.

The truth is that relatively few individuals, like Warren Buffet, for example, are fully qualified to bear the title of chief executive officer. It can be a wonderful experience ghostwriting for a senior executive, to be trusted as a confident and advisor by a distinguished leader. On the other hand, it is important to know that boards of directors have a real challenge finding individuals to trust not to lie to the board or shareholders, have sexual affairs with subordinates, contractors or consultants, use corporate funds in ways that are questionable, but not illegal, that use abusive language or make public statements offensive to customers or cultural segments of society.

Behavior is anything but predictable, even in chief executives. Former CEO of Boeing, Jim McNerney, for example, apologized in a memo to employees for telling analysts that he won't retire after turning 65 because "the heart will still be beating, the employees will still be cowering." Microsoft CEO Satya Nadella said he was "wrong" on women's pay. He suggested women shouldn't ask for raises, but rather trust that the system will take care of them. Also serious: Martin Shkreli became the symbol for price gouging after his company, Turing Pharmaceuticals, raised the price of a 62-year-old drug it had acquired to $750 a pill from $13.50. Former Peanut Corp. executive, Stewart Parnell, got a 28-year sentence for his role in a deadly salmonella outbreak. CEO, at the time, Martin Winterkorn, said Volkswagon had "broken the trust of our customers and the public" in its attempt to make millions of diesel cars appear cleaner than they are, and Ex-Goldman Sachs director Rajat Gupta was convicted of conspiracy and three counts of securities fraud. Most recently, OxyContin maker Purdue Pharma and the Sackler family that owns the company reached a tentative settlement agreement involving more than 2,000 lawsuits filed against the drugmaker for its involvement in the opioid epidemic, reported The New York Times and the Washington Post.

If you complete a writing assignment, such as a letter, memo or speech, for a chief executive and your work is criticized, questioned or just plain rejected, don't be quick to beat yourself up. I always say that people harbor an ignorant view of public relations until you explain what you do. Business executives receive no formal education in public relations. The irony of the public relations gap between PR and business is knowing that next to managing people and money, public relations is the most sought after skill in executive managers, according to a worldwide executive search firm, yet CEOs are in charge of public relations and control all public relations spending. Think about ways to educate senior managers.

The inability of many CEOs to do business in the public interest is illustrated in scandals and cover-ups in virtually all segments of business. Examples are found all over the Internet. For example, success of the asbestos companies hinged on keeping the health risks of asbestos a secret to workers and consumers who paid the price. Volkswagen CEO, at the time, Martin Winterkorn, paid the price of losing his job after it was revealed that software designed to circumvent emission testing was installed on as many as 500,000 "clean diesel" VW vehicles sold in the US and as many as 11 million worldwide. He said, "I am endlessly sorry" the brand is tarnished. Too many executives talk about corporate responsibility, integrity and putting customers first, but can't bring themselves to put ethics over profits. Enron, once seen as one of the world's most innovative companies, built its success on a scam, with the company lying about its profits and concealing bad debts in shell companies. In crisis situations, it's a wonder why companies don't seem to learn the lessons of others. Instead, CEOs look to right and wrong actions taken by their peers. Warren Buffet described managerial failings as the "institutional imperative," that is, the tendency of executives to mindlessly imitate the behavior of their peers, no matter how foolish it may be to do so.

The person with the title, "Chief Executive Officer," usually holds the highest office in an organization, over a president or chairman of the board. In many cases, you will see the title CEO coupled with president and/or board chairman. Let's take a look at a CEO's responsibilities and duties. As we examine the CEO's job, make note of the various ways public relations writing can contribute to a CEO's success. A CEO is responsible to the board of directors for everything—success or failure of an organization, its culture, compliance with laws and regulations, financing, strategic planning, operations, marketing, human resources, sales, public relations, all aspects of the business. The buck stops with the CEO. These ultimate responsibilities cannot be delegated.

Duties, on the other hand, are actions taken by a CEO. The main duty is setting a direction for an organization—having a vision and strategy that enables everyone to work toward its development and achievement. This involves hiring a senior management team to steer the organization, setting budgets, forming partnerships. It involves deciding how the organization will differentiate itself for the benefit of all stakeholders.

Another duty is establishing a culture that attracts and retains talented, skilled and motivated people, instills pride and wins loyalty to the organization and its mission. The CEO's presence or absence, action or inaction, attitude toward successes and failures, management or mismanagement of critical situations, giving recognition or steeling recognition, selfless or selfish acts, all send messages throughout an organization that shape or dismantle a business.

Another duty is team building. The CEO hires, fires and leads the senior management team. The team hires, fires and leads the rest of the organization. The CEO must be decisive in giving performers opportunities to develop and exercise their abilities and in weeding out non-performers. The CEO keeps the senior team working together, helps them resolve differences, and keep a sharp eye on the organization's vision, enabling everyone to share in the organization's progress. Team building requires establishing a code or conduct with values that will uphold the organization's reputation in all situations.

Another duty of the CEO is capital allocation. The CEO sets budgets, funds projects that contribute to the organization's strategic vision and ramps down and/or eliminates projects the lose or waste money. Some CEOs feel more comfortable in the area of financial management than others, but it's a big part of a responsibility that cannot be delegated.

From the description of the CEO's responsibilities and duties, you should feel pleasantly overwhelmed by the many opportunities there are to be of service to executives with your public relations writing skills. Here's a summary of opportunities:

- Communicate vision.
- Communicate strategies.
- Communicate brand.
- Communicate culture.
- Communicate values.
- Communicate decisions.
- Communicate achievements.

Hopefully, this presentation gave you a down-to-earth, unvarnished look at the character, abilities, responsibilities and duties of executives, the importance of maintaining your independent thinking, and the many ways you can be of service to senior managers with public relations writing.

CHAPTER 39.

ASK YOUR LEADER TO GIVE YOUR ORGANIZATION A WRITING TEST

Good writing can improve profitability

How can something as basic as good writing impact financial performance? Here are six ways to start thinking about it.

1. **Customer Service** Why are customer service costs as high as they are? Don't ask the customer service department; its aim is not to reduce or eliminate itself. Make your own assessment. Is the volume of customer calls high because product instruction sheets are unclear; because product manuals fail to adequately explain product features; because special offers, discounts, or ordering procedures are confusing? The aim should not be to improve customer service, but rather to reduce the need for it with more clearly written materials.

2. **Web Presence** Why hasn't your Web site reduced expenses as you originally expected? You set up a station somewhere in cyberspace thinking that it was going to save you money. Instead you find that customers are like shooting stars. They can appear at your cyber space station as quickly as they can disappear from it. Why? If they can't find what they're looking for quickly, they can go instantly to competing sites to find what they want. The aim should be to have your Web site content messages written so well that customers can easily find and navigate to exactly what they want.

3. **Competitive Information** Why aren't employees sharing information that could benefit the company? Intelligence that employees acquire in doing their jobs can be extremely valuable to your business. In fact, most of the competitive information you might like to have is probably right

under your own roof. The aim should be to show employees how to write to encourage interpersonal communication and greater sharing of information throughout the organization.

4. **Stock Value** Why aren't investors recognizing the full value of your company? Your company's most valuable assets are its core competencies. If you ask industry analysts, investors and potential investors to name your company's core competencies, could they do it? The aim should be to ensure that written materials communicate strategically with financial audiences.

5. **Competitive Bids** Why haven't you been winning a greater number of business bids? When no one asks a single question after your company's sales presentations, is it because the presentations are so thorough as to answer every conceivable question? Or is it because they didn't stimulate any interest? The aim should be to have presentations and proposals written that are highly persuasive and compelling enough to win new business.

6. **Quality Control** Why are your error rates higher than they should be? If you asked each of your employees to describe what is meant by "quality" in your particular operation, would you hear one concise definition, consistently, throughout the organization? Or would each person have a different idea of what is meant by quality in your organization? The aim should be to have standards clearly written and understood by the entire organization.

I have raised questions about profitability in six areas of your business. You won't find answers to my questions in financial statistics, such as return on investment, net earnings and total debt to invested capital. You don't need to hire an MBA from Harvard to find the answers. You just need to give your company a "writing test." Make a simple assessment in each area covered above, asking yourself or your customers, securities analysts, investors and other important audiences, "How well is it written?"

Assess your company's writing skills and how effectively they are applied, then take steps to raise the bar to its highest level of proficiency. You are likely to find more than one significant opportunity to improve profitability through good writing.

CHAPTER 40.

ADVISE EXECUTIVES IN ADVANCE TO LEAD WITH COMPASSION

When you least expect it, you could find yourself wishing that you had talked to your leader in advance about compassion. Consider this scenario. As a public relations staffer, you are called on to accompany your leader to where a plant, employees and their families were devastated by a hurricane. You and your executive are about to meet some employees who lost family members and personal property. Your leader greets employees, asking, "So what's the damage to the plant and how much is there?" Too late to counsel your leader on compassion. All you can do now is tag along and observe the pain of those who are suffering significant losses. This chapter is about actions you need to take now, to keep from falling into a helpless situation of tagging along and painfully watching your senior executive fail to connect with distressed employees.

What is the first thing employees want from top management following a life-threatening incident? Executives rush to the scene of a disaster, as they believe they should, and misdirect their attention to business. They meet with employees face to face and are not sure what to say, so they ask about material damage to buildings, plant and equipment. They don't think about their own creed that employees are their most important asset. When employees experience something that severely threatens their health and safety and the lives of family members, what they want is compassionate understanding.

With overbearing feelings of loss from a horrible experience locked up inside, what would employees most appreciate? What could an employer say that would make them feel better? What would employees want to be asked by their leader? More than anything else, victims suffering severe trauma want to be asked: How are you doing? How is your family? What was it like? What did you do? Every employee will have a story they feel a need to tell.

Leaders have found that some employees in a crisis, have secured their families first and returned to the workplace to secure what they could to mitigate its destruction. Those stories, when shared not just with management, but with all employees strengthen an entire organization. There is great strength to be derived for an entire organization through sharing experiences. Following a crisis, one leader sent the company's publications editor to the scene immediately after a disaster to meet with employees, listen to their stories of what happened and how they and their families were affected. The editor took pictures, recorded comments, developed a timeline of events and published the employee experience as an electronic presentation to share with and bolster the strength and pride of the organization's employees throughout the world.

Crisis is a time to put "Employees First." It's a time to exercise leadership with compassion. Attention is not going to make damaged plant and equipment magically be fixed , but it will put an organization's employees on a path to recovery.

Here's the lesson point for public relations staffers. Acknowledge to yourself that compassion isn't top of mind for most business leaders. It's business first. So waiting to talk to your leaders about the importance of compassion on the way to a disaster scene is not going to allow enough time to influence behavior in dealing with a crisis situation. Don't wait. Find time in advance to impress your leader that compassion is an important leadership quality. Advise executives that authentic leaders seek to be recognized for qualities of the heart. Bill George, former chairman and CEO of Medtronic, in his book, Authentic Leadership, wrote:

Developing your heart means following your own path and being open to all of life's experiences. It means being in touch with the depths of your inner being and being true to yourself. It requires that you know who you are, your weaknesses as well as your strengths. It is in developing compassion that we become authentic human beings.

CHAPTER 41.

REDUCE STAKEHOLDER ANXIETY WITH CORPORATE SOCIAL RESPONSIBILITY

What CSR can do for CEOs

People are restless, irritable, tense, unfocused, fatigued, sleep deprived, not just over the infamous 2016 election, but over a range of worries about an uncertain future. All of this seems to be giving way to common psychological disorders.

I wonder if CEOs appreciate how corporate social responsibility (CSR) might be helping stakeholders cope with today's rising levels of anxiety.

If corporate social responsibility could be measured and assessed relative to profitability, especially in these challenging times, I think that some CEOs would quickly raise their interest in the potential values inherent in *treating key stakeholders responsibly*, a definition by CSR authority Michael Hopkins.

In my opinion CSR is not a matter of creating a new position or department. It's about establishing a culture in which all stakeholder groups can take pride, comfort and sustainable confidence. It's about creating an environment that welcomes all stakeholders to interact, communicate, share, reach over, cooperate with civility toward each other and enjoy working on a foundation of mutually-treasured values. Walking into company facilities should feel like an experience that makes stakeholders, as well as visitors, say, "I like it here."

It's the duty of a CEO to shape the culture of an organization. I believe a CEO can create a CSR culture that triggers in all stakeholders convictions to act in support of an organization's goal or mission. But betting on CSR requires commitment from every board member and is a risk that many CEOs might be hesitant to take. Some would probably prefer to play it safe, managing costs and fine-tuning strategies. Some would prefer to mark time, waiting for things to change and hopefully improve. Some might espouse CSR but do little more than account for it as a line item.

CSR can be likened to a CEO's vision for an organization. Launching CSR is like launching a ship. If you don't know how to score the champagne bottle so it will break against the ship's hull at the christening ceremony, the result could be an embarrassing clunk, instead of a spectacular splash. In other words, if you don't know how to launch CSR, you could end up with an embarrassing disappointment rather than a shower of accolades.

I think some executives believe that CSR can be assigned to someone else. But the CEO must plant the seed and be a visible leader in fostering the seed's development. That means stepping up to others in sharing the concept and possibly being challenged, debated or criticized over its potential or validity. Without the CEO's visible leadership CSR will be no more than a pipe dream.

There is no inherent certainty for a leader that what he or she has in mind for CSR, especially in its embryonic state, is clearly right for the organization. I think executives must have the courage to engage board members in constructive discussion. They must be open to on-going dialogue with others to clarify and perfect CSR that works for the organization. Ideas are fragile. They're not complete. They're not perfect. An organization must pursue all of the pathways of human understanding necessary to affect the actions of all stakeholders who have a potential interest in the organization's success. Establishing CSR cannot be done by directive. I strongly believe it must be a culture, an achievable condition that generates positive convictions to act.

The aim of CSR shouldn't be to shoot for the moon. Its aim should be to orchestrate readily available resources to achieve results that move an organization to a higher level of innovation, competitive strength, market position and profitability. It should not be a one-sided initiative. I think it has to provide mutual benefits for stakeholders within and outside the organization. An astute leader knows that once crafted, CSR must be delivered, but not by a "town crier." It's not an edict. It's a culture.

As CSR is assimilated and evidence of its potential develops, CSR gains validity and should energize employees to produce, customers to buy, investors to invest, bankers to lend, analysts to recommend, journalists to write and communities to support. Most of all it should provide stakeholders some relief from today's mounting anxiety.

CHAPTER 42.

SHOW EXECUTIVE MANAGERS HOW TO BUILD CULTURAL COMPETENCE

Alex Levine Photography

The photo of a three-year-old girl affectionately holding what she wanted most for Christmas, a black baby doll, was chosen to depict an ultimate state of cultural competence.

The term culture is getting attention more than ever before. It has always been regarded as a strong influence over people, characterized simply as the way things are done. But now we are looking at it from a global perspective. We are recognizing the world as a culturally diverse global community. We can't ignore that differences exist between groups of people, nor can we pretend that cultures don't matter. They do. They affect our views, values, hopes, loyalties, worries and fears. Executive leaders are responsible to their boards, or should be, for the state of their organizations' culture. After all, culture is the foundation for the manner in which groups of people are managed and is reflected in the strategies, structures, systems and technology that ultimately become products and services.

Cultural competence is the ability to interact effectively with people of different cultures. If we are to counsel and assist executives in building cultural competence, we need to think about this first as individuals and professionals. We need to examine how we feel, personally, about our ability to interact effectively with people of different cultures. How, for example, would we rate our own cultural competence, say, on a scale of 1 to 10 high. Would we want to strive for an even higher score and how we could do that.

What about those we serve as professionals? All organizations have cultures, but not everyone fosters cultural competence. Some could do much better at bringing together awareness of different groups of people and having that reflected in operating standards, policies, and practices.

How would you rate the cultures of organizations, employers, clients with whom you affiliate? How would rank those affiliations in cultural competence on a scale of 1 to 10 high? Do you feel a responsibility, as a person, as a professional, to help raise those scores? While seldom talked about, public relations professionals have power and influence over the clients and employers we serve. We prepare communications in the persona, tenor, voice and style of those who lead organizations. We write remarks, make content suggestions and craft quotes in ways that reflect the cultures of organizations.

Think of how we could use our power and influence to help executive managers build culturally competent operations, how we could help them assess their organizations' cultures, help them successfully deal with and develop solutions to issues and problems created by cultural differences. We can help change how people think about other cultures, how they communicate, and how they operate. We can help executive managers and directors develop structure, leadership, and activities that reflect the kind of culture they want to see in their organizations' values, perspectives, styles, and priorities. This is much more than image building. It can only be done with the commitment of a board of directors and its executive officer to build cultural competence, assess its development, celebrate progress and share pride in diversity among all stakeholders.

We could and should make cultural competence part of our practice as individuals and public relations professionals.

CHAPTER 43.

GROWING NEED FOR ONLINE COMMUNITY ENGAGEMENT SERVICES

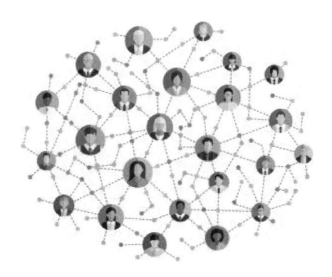

What is community engagement?

Community engagement refers to the connections between governments, citizens and communities on a range of policy, program and service issues. It encompasses a wide variety of government community interactions ranging from information sharing to community consultation, and, in some instances, active participation in government decision making processes. It takes a commitment to engagement, openness and transparency delivered through three principles:

1. informing: strengthening citizen's rights of access to information, establishing a pro-disclosure culture among government through online innovation, and making government information more accessible and usable;

2. engaging: collaborating with citizens on policy and service delivery to enhance the processes of government and improve desired outcomes; and,

3. participating: making government more consultative and participative.

What is online community engagement?

Online community engagement is any form of community engagement that occurs in the online medium. Opportunities to engage online are shaped by the technologies available and community preferences for how they want to be engaged. Over the last few years, the online environment has changed to enable individuals to create, share and engage with web content rather than being a passive recipient of content.

Why engage online?

Online community engagement can encourage greater participation in engagement activities by providing additional avenues for people to make their views known to the government which are less limited by constraints such as place, time, mobility and other access restrictions. Both government and the public benefit from greater participation—a high level of public involvement means that policy can be developed with the benefit of a wide range of different opinions and evidence. The cost and speed of processing large volumes of feedback is also significantly reduced when using online community engagement methods. People are online and want to engage with government online.

The finest application of the concept described above is in the State of Queensland and deserves global recognition for its leadership in public engagement. Visit the Queensland model:

The Outstanding Queensland Model

https://www.qgcio.qld.gov.au/documents/online-community-engagement-policy

Online community engagement should be of great interest to public relations professionals because the need for communication services in this area is rapidly trending upward. You will find, however, that many veteran public relations practitioners are yet to get an accurate grasp of the concept and, instead, easily pass it off as some traditional form of community relations. Far from it! Online community engagement is an emerging and challenging concept enabling people to better coexist. Online communication is an alternative to traditional public protest tactics characterized by crowds of demonstrators, TV news attractions, signs, loudspeaker messages. This chapter will use an actual protest campaign to illustrate the dire need for people to work together effectively.

To bring this concept to life, let's focus on an actual protest campaign that took **four years** to resolve in favor of a community of residents. We will briefly review and critique the case to illustrate the need for online community engagement.

Case Example

The place: Vancouver, Wash., U.S.A. The Port of Vancouver's board of commissioners decided to take on private partners and build the nation's biggest oil terminal to be situated on the north shore of the Columbia River across from the city of Portland, Oregon. The mission of this, and the state's 75 port districts, is to use revenue from port district taxes and develop profitable industry and trade. Residents of a district pay a port tax. The boundaries of the district in this case are those of the city.The tax rate is set by the district. The three port commissioners in Vancouver are elected by the district and serve six-year terms.

Residents and city officials opposed the terminal project and for four years used all means available to stop it. The project came close to reaching the ultimate decision maker, the governor of the state, who has the authority to approve or disapprove port projects. The port commissioners were accused correctly of working behind closed doors with their private partners in violation of open meeting and other procedural laws. Port commissioners appeared to stand in defiance of the public interest with little regard for the greater good. Commissioners claimed to be doing their jobs—using public funds to run a business and ensure profitability—as described in the Washington Public Port Association's guide for new port commissioners and state laws establishing ports and the Washington Public Ports Association.

Case Critique

Port district decisions and elections don't attract a lot of public attention until ports pursue mega projects with great potential impacts on public safety and the environment. If people don't agree with a port's position or direction, one option is to wait for six years and replace their elected commissioners. The names of commissioners might change, but the economic development mission stays the same—develop industry and trade at a profit. Another option is to express opposition to a project with public demonstrations. There is nothing in state law that obligates ports to work cooperatively with its community. A port's only obligation is to keep the public informed of its activities, for example, "By the way, we decided to build the nation's largest oil facility right here in Vancouver, or coal terminal, right here in Longview, Washington." That, essentially, leaves a port responsible to itself, certainly not to its host city, like Vancouver, or to its constituents who pay a port tax and elect commissioners, or to people affected by port decisions but live outside the port district's boundary and have no vote.

Port commissioners could take the initiative to facilitate online community engagement in their decisions, or the governor could update the state of democracy in the State of Washington by requiring community engagement. Or the public could be left with old school activities, such as public demonstrations, rallies and marches. But those tactics rarely lead expeditiously to tangible or lasting outcomes, and often heighten conflict. Government officials, generally, are stressed over the huge disconnect between local decision makers and the public, particularly as illustrated in this case. There is a real need for broad-based, constructive public participation and collaboration with government. Effective community engagement with government is happening in California, other states and other countries. However, people must be willing to hold themselves accountable to higher standards of public participation.

CHAPTER 44.

BUILD ONLINE NETWORKS TO REACH INFLUENCERS

PREPARE MEET GREET CONVERSE

There are many ways to and reasons for building online networks to reach influencers. The Internet makes it technically easy to find, connect, disconnect, like, tap responses, acquire followers, follow and unfollow. You can develop a profile that says, "Hey, look at me." You can post articles, "Here's something you want to read." You can initiate conversations, "Here's what I think?" You can randomly connect with members and boast about the number of people following you. But this type of communication has no direction and is mostly done for personal enjoyment. For the purpose of this chapter, we will focus on interpersonal rather than technical considerations because, as you will see, interpersonal factors are key to reaching online influencers within and outside organizations. They are prerequisites for success.

Building a network to reach influencers requires that you effectively prepare, meet, greet and converse.

Prepare

- Know what you bring to the table
- Have a clear objective (*Example objectives: within an organization To cause influentials to take notice of what you do, hear what you have to say and champion your value. Outside an organization, To entice influentials to review your new book and have an educated view of how to build online networks.*)
- Define the type of influencers you need to reach to achieve your objective
- Concentrate on a small number of highly qualified connections
- Headline yourself in a way that gives visitors rea-

sons to want to meet you

Meet

- Reach out as you would in making friends
- Enable them to know you and why you are contacting them
- Give them reasons to want to get acquainted
- Point out your mutual interests

Greet

- Be personable
- Be responsive and timely in your interactions
- Show that you care and value their acquaintance
- Tell them what you hope to gain from the connection
- Tell them what you hope they will gain from the connection
- Write articles and posts of mutual interest and call attention to them
- Seek their views and opinions

Converse

- Be approachable
- Welcome notices from others
- Take advantage of opportunities to be friendly, personal, polite

- To requests to join your network: I'm pleased (to connect, to know you, to make your acquaintance, etc.)

- To "likes": Thank you for your (feedback, interest, appreciation, etc.) Glad you liked my post or article. Thanks.

- In asking to be connected, or to join: I would very much like to connect because (reason).

- In asking for a connection: I have viewed your profile. We have some common interests and I would like to connect with your network.

- In accepting a new connection: I would be pleased to make your acquaintance. Or, I would be happy to have you in my network.

- In being accepted as a follower, Thank you for the opportunity (to join or follow you or your career, interests, activities, etc.)

• Be open, honest—no veiled leads into selling something (bait & switch tactic).

• Communicate when you have something of substance to convey and write for complete understanding. No one is impressed with or appreciative of a continuing stream of bothersome messages or with someone plugging up their network with casual posts.

• Show that you care about and value your connections

- Show how you can be helpful to them
- Show a sincere interest in what they do and have to say

CHAPTER 45.

IS THERE A SEAT IN THE BOARDROOM FOR THE PUBLIC INTEREST?

Mt. Druitt Standard

Communities often have issues with and raise cane with big companies. Such high emotion cries out the question, Is there a seat in the boardroom for the public interest? This question should make you think about the public interest and where and how in business it should be rooted. I don't think the gap in trust between big business and the public will be closed until the public is invited into the boardroom. Board members comprise the conscience of a corporation. Their individual thoughts and actions are hidden from view, yet they shape the culture of huge organizations.

Transparency should not stop at the doors to the boardroom. The public needs to know from each director whether or not the company **permits** them to think beyond profitability, to act socially responsible.

The public needs to know whether or not the company **requires** each director to consider the impact of its operational moves on communities and the environment.

The public needs to know from each director whether or not their **affiliations** are broad enough to expand their thinking about the benefits of serving society for a purpose greater than making money.

This transparency cannot be achieved by a chief executive

officer or public relations spokesperson. To win public trust, it must come from individual board members.

A question for further study: How much legal latitude is there between a corporation's fiduciary responsibility to stockholders to make a profit and its responsibility to invest in operating in the public interest?

CHAPTER 46.

CREATING IRRESISTABLE FUNDING OPPORTUNITIES

A Supervised Day At The Park

There will be occasions in public relations for you to raise money for worthy causes. This guidance can help you shine as a fundraiser. Trust your instincts in this area, think creatively over the heads of veteran fundraisers who say, "We have always done it this way."

Consider this example of how $200,000 was raised two weeks before a campaign was announced! In this example, there was a campaign committee of about 30 members. While a subcommittee worked on developing a fundraising brochure, others in the campaign were so impressed with the creative way it was being done that word got into the community and $200,000 was obtained by word-of-mouth before a brochure was printed.

A key to the subcommittee's success was brainstorming a collection of "funding opportunities." Instead of the traditional approach of asking for money, members created funding opportunities with enough information that donors would see as irresistible. Paging through a brochure of irresistible funding opportunities can be like exploring a holiday gift catalog. The committee decided that each "opportunity" must include a concise description, a picture, price or price range, number available and a specific benefit to a donor (usually an appropriate form of recognition).

This is an irresistible funding opportunity from the example above:

Private Evening Showings of the international art exhibit with small group tours led by qualified docents for 100 guests from 6 to 9 p.m. Friday, Saturday and Sunday with a sign on an easel in the gallery, "Private Showing of the International Art Exhibit Compliments of (Donor's Company Name)" and accommodations for a reception or after tour social gathering catered compliments of the donor. Available are 30 private showings [between dates] for a donation of $1000 each. [photo of gallery]

Sample writing of irresistible funding opportunities:

- *Summertime Reading Books* for 12 children [description] with your name as donor on a book-plate inside each book [recognition]; $50 to $60 [price/price range] for each of three sets available [availability] opportunities. [photo of children]

- *Jaws of Life* hydraulic rescue tool [description] as one of 10 donors to have a family picture taken and displayed on a thank you plaque on display in the fire house [recognition], a funding opportunity for 10 families [available] at $500 each [price].

- *Table place cards or name cards* [description] for an event with your firm's name [cards compliments of] printed prominently on each card [recognition]. One opportunity available [availability] at $500 [price] .

- *Private Backstage Party* to meet the leading lady following a performance [description]. Places for 40 guests [availability] at $50 a person [price] with all proceeds benefitting the sponsoring organization.

- *Supervised Days At A Park* with lunch for 25 children of single parents enabling them to attend job interview training [description]. Five opportunities available [availability]—one day at $450 each [price] with a welcome banner: Kids' Day With (your organization's name) [recognition].

Catalog irresistible funding opportunities with themes into mailers, fliers, posters

- Funding Opportunities For The Holidays
- Funding Opportunities At The Fire House
- Funding Opportunities To Assist Job Seekers
- Funding Opportunities To Spur Summer Reading
- Funding Opportunities For The Community Theater
- Funding Opportunities To Thank Veterans

Writing a campaign goal

Creating a fundraising campaign requires a plan with a goal. A word about crafting an effective goal. A fundraising goal should have a very strong emotional appeal. So many don't. Instead they target an amount of money to be raised. Example: Our goal is to raise $500,000. Is there anything emotionally exciting or motivating about $500,000? This is not a goal. It's an objective that tells what is needed to accomplish a goal, say, of being able to care for 12 more children in an expansion of a children's hospital. What good is a goal if you can't imagine what it will be like when the goal has been achieved? Feel the emotion in a goal making a contribution so that more children can be cared for in an expanded facility? So many fundraising plans result in disappointments because the plans lack emotional appeal, are vague, unstructured and approved not with confidence, but in hopes that they will win the trust and support of enough contributors to be considered a success or, at least, a good try. Think over the heads of veteran fundraisers? Write a goal with extraordinary emotional appeal.

CHAPTER 47.

CHECKLIST FOR SERIOUS FUND RAISING

Foundations and businesses receive hundreds of requests to fund programs, projects and organizations. Many requests are turned down because fund seekers think more about their needs than those of fund providers. You might find the checklist in this article useful in orienting your attention to fund providers. The providers of funds have as great a need for information as fund seekers have for getting contributions. But needs must be met on both sides to have a successful charitable negotiation.

Foundations and businesses want to make charitable investments with confidence. They provide guidelines that can help ensure that you instill such confidence in what you have to propose. It is essential to study guidelines before preparing requests and to fulfill the information requirements to the fullest extent possible. The following checklist, nowhere near complete, will remind you to think about *Contributors' Interests*; *Contributors' Levels of Interest*; *Proposal Content*; *Proposal Format*; and *Proposal Writing*.

PART I. CONTRIBUTORS' INTERESTS

Foundation guidelines might say, for example, we **do not** fund:

- national health organizations;
- religious groups for denominational or sectarian purposes;
- special occasions;
- goodwill advertising;
- organizations not eligible for tax-deductible support;
- endowments;
- capital projects;
- operating expenses.

We **do fund**:

- youth programs;
- health maintenance;
- music;
- culture and the arts;
- preserving the past and enhancing the future;
- education;
- people needs;
- senior citizens;
- free enterprise;
- family values.

Businesses are likely to favor proposals that:

- benefit one of the company's operating locations;
- benefit customers, employees, or communities in which they operate;
- have a Federal tax exempt certificate;
- provide services not provided by government.

PART II. CONTRIBUTORS' LEVELS OF INTEREST

Levels could be expressed, for example, in general terms, such as *recognize, reward, support,* or *invest.* For example, is the fund seeker asking a contributor to *invest* a major amount of money, when the contributor has stated that its interest is to *recognize* a worthy initiative with a small amount of seed money?

PART III. PROPOSAL CONTENT

(Note numbers of items that need to be added to your proposal.)

1. Need or problem? Why it exists? Who does it affect? How?

2. Is timing critical?

3. Is the need widely recognized?

4. Has anyone tried to address it? What was accomplished?

5. Is the need or problem accurately assessed?

6. Is the assessment supported by solid data? Is the data provided by competent sources?

7. What is the proposed solution?

8. Is the proposed solution in line with the organization's mission?

9. Is commitment to the solution in line with the organization's vision?

10. Is confidence in the solution supported by the organization's beliefs?

11. How is the proposed solution different from previous efforts to address the need?

12. What lessons were learned in past efforts that might help ensure the success of the current proposal?

13. Does the fund-seeking organization have the capacity to address the need?

14. Does the proposal include others, such as a coalition, alliance, partnership or collaboration to expand or strengthen its capabilities?

15. Can the need be addressed in the time specified?

16. How will the solution provide enduring benefits?

17. What is the strength of the organization's management capabilities?

18. Are any employees or major customers involved in the fund seeker's organization?

19. Is this request endorsed by any of the company's local operations?

20. Who benefits from the fund seeker's organization?

21. Will a contribution from the contributor make a significant difference in the success of the fund-seeker's organization?

22. Are the fund seeker's services duplicated by anyone else?

23. What are the unforeseen consequences to the contributor from a failed program?

24. Will a charitable contribution benefit the business in terms of desirable publicity, influence of certain individuals, employee recruitment, marketing, sales and goodwill?

PART IV. PROPOSAL FORMAT

Proposals should be in formats specified. There are good reasons for grant providers to specify formats. Formats facilitate:

- expediency in working with multiple reviewers,

- consistency in evaluating requests,

- fairness in comparing similar requests.

Fund seekers should format proposals exactly as specified, no matter how strongly they might disagree with the specifications. If no format is specified, one should be used that is businesslike in structure and terms.

PART V. PROPOSAL WRITING

- Organization/Style—quick read for reviewers with correct grammar, punctuation, spelling

- Readability—text completely understandable; familiar terms; no jargon; totally self-explanatory

- Accurate and correct use of terms (i.e. goal, objectives, strategies, activities)

- Positive approach

- Actions presented as opportunities

- Built on success

- Inspires confidence; reflects credibility

- Crystal clear grasp of need or problem

- Proposed actions in line with the fund-seeking organization's vision, mission, beliefs and history

- Identity, purpose, validity of the fund-seeking organization

- One-page program/project description

- Realistic program budget

- Timeline
- Member criteria and data
- Letters of community and other sources of support
- Board member names
- Names of officers
- Organization's budget and audited financial statement

CHAPTER 48.

THINK OF DONORS AS 'LOST PATRONS'

Many development professionals are doing the right things when it comes to retaining donors for the long term. Some, however, are taking established donors for granted, and that's what puts donors on a fast track to becoming lost patrons. If you are advising or directing an organization that is dependent on donors, you will benefit from knowing what I call the Lost Patron Syndrome and what actions to take to guard against it.

Why view donors as lost patrons?

By seeing donors as lost patrons, you will be constantly reminded to fight the Lost Patron Syndrome (LPS) and keep donors for longer times. Having worked with the nonprofit sector, I believe the Lost Patron Syndrome has distinct stages:

- One stage is when donors have a strong connection, both personal and physical, with an organization, like a university or charity.

- The next stage is when donors become geographically separated from an organization and begin to have a diminishing personal connection through attrition of friends and acquaintances at the organization.

- The next stage is when donors are both geographically and personally separated from an organization and their connection is, at best, distant and other organizations are competing for attention and support.

- The last stage is when donors stop contributing and become "lost patrons."

What can organizations do to guard against Lost Patron Syndrome?

It is essential to recognize LPS, refuse to accept it as a normal phenomenon, and make a conscious decision to strengthen efforts to stay connected with loyal donors as long as possible. Many organizations take existing donors for granted in favor of focusing on attracting, winning and catering to new donors. There are many things organizations can do to retain and keep donors for longer periods of time:

- One thing they can do is ensure that communication with donors is always genuine. Sending a message and pretending that a VIP is personally acquainted with a donor is clearly seen as disingenuous. A thank you message from a VIP addressed to all donors is seen as genuine.

- Another thing an organization can do if a donor's contribution was, for example, in support of a student, is to have the student hand-write and send the thank you note.

- Another thing an organization can do at a fundraising event is ensure that donor guests are recognized, greeted, never left unattended, and personally thanked for attending.

- Another thing an organization can do to help keep connections alive is provide donors with images that preserve treasured memories, images of things when they were fully connected.

Other things organizations can do to prevent LPS:

Organizations must always deliver what they promise donors. Telling donors their names will be listed in a program and not including them is a broken promise.

Organizations can evoke pride among donors by highlighting achievements of other donors and the organization. Evoking pride is best done by message points that are short and conversational—in a form easily conveyed to others.

Another thing organizations can do to fight LPS is establish two-way online engagement with donors. Use an interactive platform to call on donors as resources for papers, opinions on issues, comments on various aspects of planning fundraising activities.

Organizations also should call on and use donors as "rainmakers"—close friends of potential donors.

By seeing donors as lost patrons, you will be constantly reminded to fight Lost Patron Syndrome and keep donors for longer times.

CHAPTER 49.

ATTRACT AND RETAIN A WHOLE CADRE OF VOLUNTEERS

You can attract a whole cadre of volunteers to serve an organization by providing volunteer experiences that evoke feelings of joy and gratification that individuals can't wait to describe to others. In too many cases, individuals come eager to help and leave disappointed and not likely to return. But when the experience is fulfilling, individuals want to talk about it. They will speak with contagious enthusiasm that infects others and motivates them to pursue the same experience.

A volunteer experience can offer personal growth, giving people a chance to learn new skills, develop additional capabilities and discover more about themselves. A volunteer experience can be a valuable outlet for developing relationships. It can be a place for meeting new friends and providing a feeling of belonging and an opportunity for making social connections. Exceptional volunteer opportunities are spread by word-of-mouth that enables an organization to attract and maintain an adequate complement of volunteers. For this kind of recruitment to happen, an organization must put volunteer management on the same level as all operational functions, responsible for creating the right conditions and meeting predefined needs of volunteers.

Creating The Right Conditions

The right conditions can be summarized this way:

1. Have a work environment from the top down that welcomes, respects and appreciates volunteers.

2. Have a chief executive who holds himself or herself accountable for volunteerism—to ensure that policies for its engagement are effectively managed throughout the organization.

3. Include how to treat volunteers in the organization's job descriptions

4. Have in place all of the resources necessary for

volunteers to have an exceptional experience.

5. Have practices that ensure that volunteered time is continually put to good use.

6. Have assignments ready that are well-defined, interesting and relevant to a volunteer's interests and needs.

7. Have assignments that give all volunteers a clear opportunity to accomplish something and see direct results of their efforts.

What A Volunteer Needs

Predefined, universal needs of volunteers can be summarized this way:

1. A job description stating tasks to be done, work standards, measurements and reporting relationships

2. A job title for use in a resume

3. Introduction to staff members

4. Job orientation to the physical layout use of an organization's space

5. Work area and necessary tools

6. List of co-workers with job titles, phone numbers and reasons why they are important to the volunteer

7. Useful publications and documents to read

8. A conversation about how assignments contribute to the volunteer's professional goals

9. Periodic, formal critiques of the volunteer's performance

10. Notes of praise that the volunteer could include in a job portfolio

11. Meaningful recognition that exceeds a mere "thank you"

12. A word of encouragement or praise for specific work

CHAPTER 50.

HOW TO SELECT A PR FIRM

Satisfaction of working with true professionals!

At some point in your career, you most likely will have an opportunity to select a public relations firm to assist you with your work. This guidance will help ensure that you don't make a mistake in your selection, ending up spending a lot of money and not getting the help you need.

Public relations firms can be divided into two categories: service-driven and cost-driven. You want to be sure you know the difference so you can make the right choice.

So what distinguishes a service-driven from a cost-driven PR firm?

1. Use of time is one distinguishing factor. Service-driven firms use time to provide service. Cost-driven firms use time to cover costs at the expense of client service. Firms become cost-driven when the cost of operating—office rent, auto and electronic equipment leases, salaries, and other overhead—is so high that meeting those expenses drives the business.

2. A service-driven firm provides a client with an experienced account representative. A cost-driven firm provides an experienced account representative, initially, then switches to a less experienced representative, but at the same high billable rate.

3. A service-driven firm provides a client with the full depth of the firm's expertise. A cost-driven firm limits client service to the experience of the account representative to allow others in the firm to concentrate on more lucrative business.

4. A service-driven firm provides a client with high-quality resources for graphic design, photography, video production and whatever is needed. A cost-

driven firm attempts to use its own, often mediocre in-house resources, to increase client billing for the firm.

5. A service-driven firm charges on the basis of its employees' abilities and experience. A cost-driven firm might try to ignore federal laws against, say, charging clients regular fees for work from unpaid interns.

6. A service-driven firm drives the client's assignment to completion. A cost-driven firm is less responsive, causing the client to do the account representative's work of staying on schedule and on budget and enables the account representative to handle more accounts.

7. A service-driven firm is willing to tailor its services to a client's direction, like asking for help in augmenting a small staff. A cost-driven firm insists on its own way of providing service and resists client attempts to manage and evaluate the firm's performance.

8. A service-driven firm keeps honest time sheets. A cost-driven firm might be tempted to ignore federal law against inflating or "padding" timesheets, as was spotlighted in the movie, "The Firm."

9. A service-driven firm knows how to support a client's work. A cost-driven firm keeps its independence and functions to its own advantage.

10. A service-driven firm keeps working until the work meets the client's expectations. A cost-driven firm offers excuses for substandard work and

sometimes tries to get the client to accept and pay for the PR firm's mistakes, inability to follow directions, poor writing, careless editing and other unprofessional practices.

Public relations firms should be working continually to strengthen the public's trust in the profession. That is a core principle of the Code of Ethics of the Public Relations Society of America (PRSA). According to the code, members of PRSA should:

- acknowledge that there is an obligation to protect and enhance the profession;
- keep informed and educated about practices in the profession to ensure ethical conduct;
- actively pursue personal professional development;
- decline representation of clients or organizations that urge or require actions contrary to the code;
- accurately define what public relations activities can accomplish; counsel subordinates in proper ethical decision making;
- require that subordinates adhere to the ethical requirements of the code;
- report ethical violations, whether committed by PRSA members or not, to the appropriate authority.

By selecting a service-driven firm, you are far more likely to get an acceptable return on your public relations investment. Enjoy your selection of a service-driven PR firm! Have fun working together with other genuine public relations professionals.

CHAPTER 51.

WHAT TO DO WHEN YOUR GRADE DEPENDS ON OTHER TEAM MEMBERS

When your grade depends on the work of all team members, it's important to get members to agree to be tough on performance right from the start. A team might seem so smooth that it could win a congeniality award, but when the workload mounts up and members start giving less than their full support to the team, your grade is at stake. You can't afford that! Following is an evaluation form used in business. Get team members to agree on something like this. No comments are allowed. Members must evaluate each other, periodically, with a 1, 2, 3, or 4. Distribute evaluations to members and have them report back to the team on what they intend to do to improve their respective evaluations.

TEAM MEMBER EVALUATION

Make a selection for each team member

1 Does the work, participates

2 Tries to do the work, participates

3 Can't do the work, doesn't participate

4 Can do the work, doesn't participate

Evaluate each team member periodically. No notes or partial scores. Just 1, 2, 3, or 4.

1 2 3 4 _____

1 2 3 4 _____

1 2 3 4 _____

1 2 3 4 _____

1 2 3 4 _____

Print name of team member evaluator and date

_____

CHAPTER 52.

A WHIMSICAL INTRODUCTION TO PUBLIC RELATIONS PLANS

The Frog Show is a whimsical introduction to the 10 components of a public relations plan. In the profession, we use strategic communication to influence behavior. This presentation uses a frog to illustrate the planning process. Even veteran practitioners have found this presentation useful in better understanding how to write public relations plans. See the show here, or for a slide presentation for group viewing, take the URL https://pressbooks.com/app/uploads/sites/66729/2018/02/FROG-SHOW.pdf.

THE FROG SHOW

A colleague said it so well: "Public relations plans should be easily understood and plausible in the minds of reviewers with the appearance of truth and reason, seemingly worthy of approval or acceptance, credible and believable." This presentation illustrates 10 components of a good public relations plan.

Plan Component #1 — PROBLEM

There is a problem. We have a frog that refuses to go back into its pond. The bank around the pond is wet and slippery and the safest time to take action would be in daylight hours. If we wait until after dark to get the frog back into the pond we run the risk of slipping, unseen, into deep water surrounded by a steep, slippery bank and no place to climb out. This problem calls for public relations—the practice of influencing behavior.

Plan Component #2 — SITUATION

Our analysis of the situation is that the frog will not respond to instructions. We have tried over and over to tell the frog to jump back into the pond. First we tried a friendly, polite approach: "Would you please jump back into the pond?" Then we tried a firm approach, "We want you to jump back into the pond." Then we became frustrated and started shouting orders. "Get back into the pond!" Based on this failed experience, we could only conclude that the frog is stubborn. Not knowing what else to do, we decided to call on professional help— a public relations expert who knows how to influence behavior.

Plan Component #3 — GOAL

A public relations expert accepted our challenge to influence the behavior of the frog. "The goal," she said, "is for the frog to be back in the pond." We said, "Yes, that's what we want."

Plan Component #4 — TARGET

"To achieve our goal, the focus of our effort must be on the frog," said the PR expert. The frog is our target.

Plan Component #5 — OBJECTIVE

According to the PR expert, an objective tells what must be done to achieve the goal and it must have three parts: 1) an action; 2) a receiver of the action; 3) and a certain behavior by the receiver that is desired as a result of the action taken. So the PR expert says that the objective should be: "To make the frog jump back into the pond before nightfall." The action is to make the frog jump. The receiver or target of the action is the frog. The desired result of the action is for the frog to jump into the pond before dark.

Plan Component #6 — STRATEGY

The PR expert explains that we need a strategy because that tells how we will achieve our objective. "Our strategy," she says, "will be to lure the frog back into the pond."

Plan Component #7 — TACTIC

The PR expert says to fully explain how we are going to carry out our strategy we will add specific tactics or activities to our strategy. She said, "Our tactic or activity will be to lure the frog with a fly connected by a thread to a twig to lead the frog back into the pond.

Plan Component #8 — EVALUATION

The success of our public relations effort to influence the behavior of the frog will be determined by observing the frog back in the pond before nightfall.

The PR expert said that our timeline will include four steps: 1) preparing to connect a fly with a thread to a twig of an appropriate shape and length; 2) approaching the frog strategically; 3) beginning the luring operation before nightfall; 4) and causing a final leap into the pond.

Plan Component #10 — BUDGET

Personnel	Rate/Hour	Estimated Hours/d	Estimated Days	
Acct. Executive	110	2	1	220.00
Assistant	95	2	1	190.00
Out of pocket Expenses				
Photography				120.00
Pictorial Report				200.00
Knife to cut twig				12.00
Spool of thread				3.00
TOTAL for influencing the behavior of a frog				745.00

A proposed budget for public relations services includes an hourly rate for personnel, plus out-of-pocket expenses. The total cost of influencing the behavior of the frog is $745.

Detailed instruction on how to write the components of a plan are provided in the book, *Writing Winning Proposals: Public Relations Cases* by Rebecca A. Gilliland and Thomas R. Hagley:

View book at Cognella Academic Publishing

Amazon Prime   Cognella Academic Publishing

View book at Amazon

CHAPTER 53.

PREPARING TO WRITE A PUBLIC RELATIONS PLAN

Rebecca A. Gilliland

Thomas R. Hagley

As co-authors of the new 3rd edition of Writing Winning Proposals: Public Relations Cases, we would like to offer advice for preparing to write public relations plans in a unique way and through an imperative lens that should be widely understood and taught. Knowing full well that not everyone who reads this chapter will peruse our book, we would like to take advantage of this ebook outlet to communicate some advice for our PR colleagues to contemplate.

Edward Bernays long advocated that public relations is indeed an applied social science and should be treated as such. He likened placing a public relations program in a communication department to teaching a surgeon only to use instruments without prior knowledge of the human body. He felt that assessing and understanding any situation, of course, preceded the use of the necessary communication tools. Furthermore, several scholars have found that business skills are seen as deficient among public relations professionals. Even the Institute for Public Relations and the Public Relations Society of America reports that entry-level professionals feel confident in their writing skills, but not so much in their business skills. This was according to a study of 386 entry-level professionals. An author of the aforementioned textbook conducted eight focus groups and found from 44 professionals that business skills, as assessed by those in more senior positions, were perceived as lacking in entry-level public relations professionals.

As stated, Bernays suggested that we assess and understand a situation before using communication tools. This is, after all, what public relations should be at its core. It's about audience analysis and communicating to an audience in a way that people will best understand the messaging. If we don't do that as PR professionals, we are not using our own advice—or our own training. Think about this…we drill our juniors on AP Style, as it's the way to speak to the media. Yet we write business proposals—to deliver to those who are trained in business—as if we are speaking to others who are trained in public relations. This is a common yet terrible error in judgement in our profession.

Do you think that writing public relations plans and proposals requires business skills? Do you think that a PR plan should be written in vocabulary that would be seen as "PR ease"? A plan is the instrument used to propose and obtain approvals from **business** clients and **business** employers of PR staffers for virtually all PR spending. Business people use them as a mechanism for monitoring and evaluating program progress and activities. The quality of plans distinguishes true PR professionals and strategists from those who are not actually utilizing their PR training while writing such proposals (they are not investigating the social science or using the business skills necessary to succeed). In view of this importance, do you feel that you need more training in business—the language in which such a plan should be written so that the receivers can best understand?

Before signing up for business courses and more degrees, there is something you can do to close the gap in confidence between PR skills and business skills. One is by writing plans that give business managers information they want, the way they want it. Writing Winning Proposals: Public Relations Cases is written entirely from a business perspective, with rules for writing every part of a public relations plan or proposal. This is basic, but not taught well enough in the classroom. Educators, as well as veteran PR practitioners, have institutionalized what they think business people want in PR plans and how they think business people want to get it. Entry-level professionals are shackled to this institutionalized perspective expressed ubiquitously in the phrase, "This is the way it's done."

There is a history of evidence showing how this institutionalized thinking of many educators and veteran public relations practitioners is holding open the gap of understanding between business people and public relations practitioners. The evidence comes right out of the mouths of reviewers in their reactions to plan presentations. For example: "You said that was a goal. Now you're calling it an objective. Or is it a strategy? I'm thoroughly confused." Some terms used in the trade, like goal and objective, are given a variety of definitions within PR. The definitions of those words widen and vary over different industries even more—industries that we are trying to communicate with. Even within the PR field itself, there are numerous definitions as to what the term "public relations" is and does. There is so much riding on the decoding of one word or term to ensure that our audience uses the same meaning that we are trying to convey.

Another example: "The goal is to obtain from public and private sources, including individuals, $5 million by conducting a capital fund drive using a capital fund drive brochure." No, this is not a goal. The statement combines an objective with a strategy and a tactic. Another example, also taken straight from a national award-winning plan: "Work on many levels of the problem simultaneously to deliver a cannon shot impact that is deep and long lasting." This is not an objective. Frankly, one can't discern what it is. Another example from an award-winning plan: "Develop key messages and create benefit-focused materials that set a celebratory tone." No, this is not a strategy; it's gobbledygook.

Finding plans good enough to compete in national competitions has for years required extensive searches. So would acquiring business skills help you as a plan writer? Or would good writing from the perspective of reviewers, providing the information they want, the way they want it, close the gap of understanding between business and public relations? Business wants just what you would want if payment for a plan was coming out of your pocket. But it's not—it's coming out of theirs. And it's time that we, as PR practitioners understand that.

Our advice is to write your plan from a business perspective. Though our advice is written primarily in PR language (for our audience is the readers who are PR-knowledgeable), please understand that the actual output—the style of writing to answer these things—should be in everyday English. Following is some guidance:

- Does the plan begin with a statement summarizing a problem, challenge, opportunity or situation which, when addressed with public relations activity, would in some significant way benefit an organization or client? Is that explained?
- Does the plan present a thorough analysis of the

situation, stopping short of suggesting solutions? Does the situation analysis give plan reviewers solid assurance that that plan developer has a complete and accurate understanding of the situation from which to develop a plan?

- Does the plan present one, and only one goal? Is it written in one sentence? Is the goal something you can imagine? Is it written as though it has been achieved—stating an ultimate condition or state of being resulting from successful execution of the plan? Acceptable: For XYZ **to be** operating as a recognized leader in its field. This is written as though the company has arrived at a new level of esteem—a new state of being. Unacceptable: The goal is for XYZ **to become** a recognized leader in its field. That leaves XYZ in its current unrecognized position or state of being—trying **to become** a recognized leader. To achieve the goal, the focus of a PR plan, without exception, must be on engaging and influencing the behavior of people—individuals and or target audiences—through strategic communication.

- Does the plan identify and describe each target audience? Does it tell why the target audiences were selected, what each one knows about the subject of the plan, how each one is positioned relative to the subject, what each one's disposition toward the plan's originating entity? Does the plan present each of the audiences separately? Or does the plan, unacceptably, just list target audiences, taking for granted that reviewers can figure out for themselves why they were selected?

- Does the plan have objectives that tell reviewers **what** must be done with each target audience to achieve the plan's goal. Does each objective start with the infinitive "To," and contain three parts: 1) an action to be taken, 2) a receiver (audience) of the action, 3) a behavior desired of the receiver as a result of the action to be taken? Is each objective written to enable measurement? *Example: To provide the media with information so they take an interest in writing articles and that their reports can be based on complete and accurate information.* Unacceptable objectives are those that include **by doing something,** which tells **how** an objective will be accomplished and that is the job of a strategy.

- Does each objective in the plan have one or more strategies? Do the strategies describe **how**, in concept, each objective is to be achieved. Do the strategies include discussions of messages or themes, or creative ideas that plan reviewers have not considered? Are the strategies presented in broad terms, stopping short of giving details as to how they will be carried out, which is the job of the plan's **activities or tactics**?

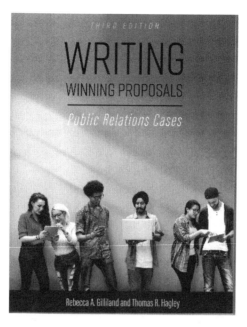

Some of the above advice may seem uncomfortable from what you have been taught in class or instructed by PR practitioners. For instance, you might write an objective based on the advice above that might fail in a classroom or entry job. But it is essential to focus on your audience of business reviewers. Keep in mind that the information you used to write the objective will still exist (in your own notes, your own documents). All that you were taught and teach to your juniors is still relevant. But in the actual *tool* that you will present to the reviewer—the plan—that audience analysis must be present. It may not be comfortable to deviate from what you learned, but it's what your business audience wants, the way business professionals want it. It's the way to write winning plans.

Rebecca Gilliland is the Distinguished Professor of Service-Learning and Associate Professor of Communication at the University of Indianapolis. Thomas Hagley is senior instructor of public relations retired from the University of Oregon.

Cognella Academic Publishing

Amazon Prime

View book at Cognella Academic Publishing

View book on Amazon

CHAPTER 54.

PRESENTING PR PLANS IN TEAMS

The way in which public relations plans are presented contributes significantly toward a plan's approval or rejection. This chapter shows how to organize a team presentation and also describes what information should be included in each of a plan's 10 components. To be effective, teams need to pay attention to organization and content of a plan, both of which are covered. By following this presentation format, your team will be able to save countless hours organizing that can be applied, instead, to rehearsing your presentation.

First let's get oriented to the parts of a public relations plan using the chart below. Then, we will assign parts of the plan to members of your team and finally we will describe the information they will be expected to present. The example is for a five-member team but can be modified to accommodate smaller or larger teams.

Public Relations Plan Diagram

INTRODUCTORY STATEMENT

SITUATION ANALYSIS

GOAL

TARGET AUDIENCE #1
Objective
Strategy
Tactic/Activity
Evaluation

TARGET AUDIENCE #2
Objective
Strategy
Tactic/Activity
Evaluation

TARGET AUDIENCE #3
Objective
Strategy
Tactic/Activity
Evaluation

TARGET AUDIENCE #4
Objective
Strategy
Tactic/Activity
Evaluation

EXECUTION TIMELINE

BUDGET

A plan begins with an introductory **statement** about a problem, opportunity or challenge. Then comes an **analysis** of the situation from which a **goal** is developed. To achieve the goal, work must be done with people, often grouped and referred to as **target audiences** or focal points. Each target audience is followed by one or more **objectives**, telling *what* must be done with each audience to achieve the plan's goal. Each objective is followed by one or more **strategies** telling *how* each objective is to be accomplished. Each strategy is followed by **tactics** or activities telling in more detail how each strategy will be implemented. Reviewers who have the authority to approve plans also want to know, specifically, how the work aimed at each target audience will be **evaluated**. Plans include **timelines** showing a schedule of work to be performed and when milestones will be reached. Last, but important, is a **budget** showing how a client will be billed for a plan. There you have an overview of the component parts of a public relations plan. Next, let's assign parts to team members. If you are wondering about the reason for this presentation format, it is designed to be easily understood by those who approve plans.

Let's say that you are the leader of a five-person team. You will present the plan's introductory statement, situation analysis, and goal. You will explain that the team has identified four target audiences for your plan. You will introduce Team Member #2, taking your time and pronouncing the person's name in a clear, audible and respectful voice, stating that this person will talk about the first target audience. Member #2 will identify and describe the target audience, explain the objective and the strategy to be pursued to achieve it. The member will explain the tactics to be used to implement the strategy and how the work in this area will be evaluated. Team Member #2 will introduce the next team member who will apply the process to target audience #3, and introduce the next team member who will cover target audience #4. You, as team leader, will wrap up the presentation covering the execution timeline and budget and asking for approval to proceed with the plan.

Parts have been assigned to team members. Now let's take a look at what team members should explain in each part.

#1   Introductory Statement

The introductory statement summarizes a problem, challenge, opportunity or situation which, when addressed with public relations activity, will in some significant, measurable way benefit the organization you work for or that you have as a client. It should be headed: Problem, Challenge, Opportunity or Situation without the words "introductory" or "statement."

#2   Situation Analysis

The situation analysis is more than a report of known facts; it is your analysis of the situation. So present the information you have as you understand it and include recommendations for further investigation (informal or formal research) into areas that you believe require clarification or verification. Write it in a conversational, storytelling style.

#3   Goal

A plan should have one goal written in one sentence. It should be distinguished by the use of the present infinitive phrase "to be," responding to the question, What do you want the ultimate condition or state of being to be as a result of having executed the public relations plan successfully? (Example: For the medical center to be serving 50 additional patients.)

#4 Target Audience (or focus)

The focus of a plan, without exception, should be on people because public relations is the practice of influencing behavior through strategic communication. Practically speaking, a plan could not be implemented without the engagement of people. A plan must focus on influencing the behavior of people to achieve the plan's goal. The focus of a plan could be on one individual, on individuals comprising an organization or segment of an organization, on individuals comprising an audience or an entire public.

#5 Objective

Objectives tell plan reviewers WHAT actions must be taken with subjects of the plan to achieve a plan's goal. More than one objective usually is needed to achieve a goal. There must be one objective for each focal point or target audience of a plan.

An objective is distinguished by starting it with the infinitive "To," and must contain three parts: 1) an action to be taken; 2) a receiver of the action (i.e. focal point, target audience); and 3) a behavior that is desired of the receiver as a result of the action taken.

Example: "To inform employees about the company's skyrocketing costs of medical insurance so that they are willing to accept an increased share of the cost."

#6 Strategy

Strategies describe HOW a plan's objectives will be achieved. Plan reviewers want to be able to assess your methods for achieving objectives, the creativity behind your methods, the feasibility and practicality of your methods, and your knowledge of applying the fundamentals of persuasion in influencing behavior.

#7 Tactic (or activities)

An activity or tactic is what puts a strategy into action. Activities provide the details of a strategy. Plan reviewers want to assure themselves that they concur with the ways in which strategies are to be carried out. More than one activity is required to implement a strategy.

#8 Evaluation

The execution time line is a schedule of all activities in a plan. The time line provides a visual—at-a-glance—sequence of actions showing how long each will take to implement.

#9 Execution Timeline

The execution time line is a schedule of all activities in a plan. The time line provides a visual—at-a-glance—sequence of actions showing how long each will take to implement.

#10 Budget

A proposed budget is developed from one of two positions: One position is that you represent a public relations firm or agency and your plan is for a client. The other position is that you are an employee of an organization with responsibility for public relations and your plan is for your employer. You must use a budget format that is appropriate for your position.

Detailed instruction on how to write the components of a plan are provided in the book, *Writing Winning Proposals: Public Relations Cases* by Rebecca A. Gilliland and Thomas R. Hagley: Amazon Prime   Cognella Academic Publishing

View book at Amazon

View book at Cognella Academic Publishing

Progress Tracking Report (Highly recommended.)

The Progress Tracking Report provides an at-a-glance visual check to show clients or employers that activities of the plan are on schedule, on target, on budget and completed or not. In too many cases, clients find themselves having to call and ask for the status of a project, when, in fact, the PR agency should be managing the account.Once a template is formed (see example) the report can be updated easily and submitted to plan reviewers on paper or electronically as frequently as desired. Offering a project tracking report shows a client or employer that the plan implementer is taking the initiative to manage the project openly and meticulously.

Progress Tracking Report (example)				
Target Audience	Activity	On schedule On target On budget (green cells)	Behind schedule and/or over budget (red cells)	Completed (blue cells)
Donors	Names	�		
	Rainmakers		▓▓	
	Brochure	▓		
	Memberships	▓		
Graduate Students	Briefings			▓▓
Undergraduate Students	Internships	▓		
	Ambassadors	▓		
	Workshop		▓▓	
	Longhouse			
Community	Inquiry		▓▓	
	Response			
	Resolution		▓▓	
	Event	▓		
	Tee-shirts	▓		
	Award	▓		
	Ceremony	▓		
	Center/City	▓		
	Honoree	▓		
University faculty & staff	Ambassador		▓▓	
	Letter #1		▓▓	
	Letter #2		▓▓	
	Website			▓▓
Donors	Survey			
	Annual report			

CHAPTER 55.

USE CPM TO PRESENT PUBLIC RELATIONS PLANS VISUALLY

Some people like to be able to visualize plans, especially when they involve many steps over an extended period of time. CPM, or the Critical Path Method, provides a graphic view of plans and is especially useful in public relations. It enables a PR practitioner to map out a plan visually, show activities and their relationship to each other, all against a timeline for their execution. It enables clients to see at a glance in a document or on an electronic presentation screen an entire plan. You can explore much more about critical path planning; however, this chapter will introduce you to the basics so you can put it to work right away as naturally as sketching notes on a napkin at Starbucks.

Let's build a structure for CPM's use in public relations. In PR we use strategic communication to influence behavior. That usually requires a series of steps over a period of time. Preparatory steps lead to achieving strategies, to the achievement of objectives or milestones and ultimately to a goal.

First, draw a timeline.

_____

Next let's add activities. What works nicely is to put achievements, milestones, or deliverables above the timeline and preparatory activities below the timeline. You could decide that strategic milestones critical to the plan will be in public view and preparatory steps leading up to them will be regarded as work behind the scenes.

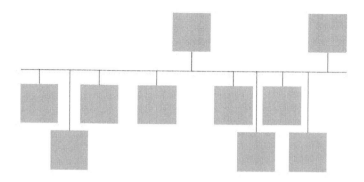

In this example, the Critical Path Method displays with dates preparatory activities below a timeline and milestones, deliverables, items critical to the success of the plan intended for public view above the timeline. Common practice is for the graphic boxes to be connected with lines to the timeline and for dates to be inserted on the timeline for each activity. To further illustrate, let's say two preparatory steps (shown below the line) are 1) committee discusses an issue, 2) committee develops message points for a representative, and a third critical activity step (shown above the line) in public view 3) representative presents message points at a town hall meeting.

CPM shows the length of a path of planned activities to milestones in public view, and the earliest and latest that each activity can start and finish without making the timeline longer. This process shows which activities are "critical" (i.e., in public view above the timeline) and which have some "float" (i.e., activities below the timeline showing how much they can be moved in either direction without affecting the critical activities).

Of particular note, use of the CPM gives plan developers a clear way to show clients and employers of PR staffs how much time and work is necessary to achieve each step in a plan. It also facilitates an understanding of the total cost and time to complete a plan.

CHAPTER 56.

FIRST MEETING WITH A CLIENT—BEFORE, DURING AND AFTER

First meeting with a client—before, during and after

The first time meeting with a client is most impressive when a public relations firm is seen operating in everything it says and does from a culture deep rooted in service. That's because the most important factor in developing business is providing good service. This chapter describes how a service-oriented firm operates before, during and after the first meeting with a client. By operating from a culture deep rooted in service, a public relations firm will soar above the rest in attracting and retaining business.

Actions prior to the first meeting

1. In preparing for the first meeting with a client, members of a service-oriented firm are reminded to be respectful of individuals of earlier (older) generations whose standards and expectations of business behavior most likely are different from today's in terms of language, humor, gestures, attire and physical appearance (e.g. hair style and color, tattoos, facial jewelry, etc.). Business is being lost every day over generational insensitivities with clients who feel uncomfortable with the way they are treated and the way business is being conducted.

2. In preparing to meet for the first time with a client, members of a service-oriented firm are reminded to discuss, not pitch, the firm's capabilities, avoiding huckster titles, like "our cyber reputation repair team," "our drives management experts," or "our dashboard engineers."

3. In preparing to meet with a new client, members of a service-oriented firm plan to have fun and enjoy the experience, while maintaining a business decorum, knowing that PR is not a take-a-number, walk-in shop run by glad-handing pitch

and spin artists. Members respect public relations as high stakes business with money and desired results on the table. All members of the firm know that clients pay thousands of dollars for public relations services, and for products, like speeches, worthy of respect, spotless reproduction and packaging.

Actions during the first client meeting

1. For the first meeting with a client, a service-oriented PR firm greets clients in an area good for "human" socializing—an area devoid of electronic devices and sounds, from phones to projection equipment. Members take time for relaxed socializing—greetings and introductions, exchange of business cards and pleasant conversation. If there is likely to be an account team, the firm will provide the new client with team member contact information, photos, full names, titles and biographical sketches. During the course of the meeting, members make a point of repeating first names distinctly and clearly. Members show clients that they now have a special place away from the office that is nice to visit.

2. Members know that to listen is more important than to talk, especially at the first meeting with a client. They give their new client ample time to describe in detail the client's need for public relations, concerns about hiring and working with a PR firm, how things will be managed, measured and billed.

3. A service oriented firm shows flexibility in putting a client's interests above its own, even if what is wanted by the client, like an extension of staff, goes against the firm's desire to be in charge of the whole show.

4. Members of a service-oriented firm, from receptionist to chief executive officer, follow an established protocol giving clients 100 percent of their presence, ruling as unacceptable behavior, actions like stepping aside and saying "I've got to take this…" "I'm needed in another conference room…" and anything else that would give a client the impression that someone or something else is more important than the guest.

5. Members of a service-oriented firm are acutely aware that not everyone is tech savvy and that many require time for definitions and explanations. In today's world people speed wiggle their thumbs to text, chat, face and paste emoji. Television news people and their guests talk over each other and spit words out like corn from a popping machine. Members of a service-oriented firm play the human side of technology.

Actions after the first meeting with a client

1. A service-oriented firm is always a step ahead of the client with the next action top of mind and work on target, on schedule and on budget. The firm always has a grasp of what might be developing that is or could be challenging to the business goal, objectives or strategies. Recommended

moves are always at the ready to suggest and for the firm to implement.

2. A service firm manages its accounts, providing regular progress reports, never leaving a client in a position of having to ask about the status of a project.

3. When a new client calls, the firm gives 100 percent of its presence. No side conversations by the receiver of the call. No keyboard or computer background noise. No "Put-you-on-hold-for-a-second" or "Please select from the following, the executive for your account and press the pound sign."

4. When a meeting is over a meal, the firm always makes the reservation, discretely picks up the bill with no hesitation and pays it, regardless of the number of guests, knowing it will be charged back as an expense to the client's account.

By operating from a culture deep rooted in service, a public relations firm will soar above the rest in attracting and retaining business.

CHAPTER 57.

WHAT CLIENTS EXPECT FROM PR ACCOUNT EXECS AND CONSULTANTS

This is what clients expect

from public relations account executives and consultants:

- professional support and expertise in helping you get work done

- flexible support from leading a project to serving as an extension of staff

- support that frees up time for you to work on other matters

- well-managed support

- 100 percent of his/her presence—without exception, no distractions or interruptions from electronic devices or anything else

- observations of the broader work environment

- close oversight of work assigned

- recommendations for modifications, changes in

direction

- regular or more reports of current status of work—timely execution, budgeting and billing

- efficient handling of logistics—reservations, transportation or directions, catering, name tags, table tent cards, meeting materials, electronic presentation and recording services, etc.

- presentable appearance, in command of social graces, always picks up the check for meals and entertainment

- status reports, client never having to ask where things stand

- Progress Tracking Report that shows at-a-glance and in bright colors by target audience, the status of all major activities in an assignment or plan. It would show that an activity is on schedule, on target, on budget; behind schedule, and/or over budget; or completed. See the sample report.

Progress Tracking Report (example)				
Target Audience	**Activity**	**On schedule On target On budget (green cells)**	**Behind schedule and/or over budget (red cells)**	**Completed (blue cells)**
Donors	Names	▓		
	Rainmakers		▓	
	Brochure	▓		
	Memberships	▓		
Graduate Students	Briefings			▓
Undergraduate Students	Internships	▓		
	Ambassadors	▓		
	Workshop		▓	
	Longhouse			
Community	Inquiry		▓	
	Response		▓	
	Resolution		▓	
	Event	▓		
	Tee-shirts	▓		
	Award	▓		
	Ceremony	▓		
	Center/City	▓		
	Honoree	▓		
University faculty & staff	Ambassador		▓	
	Letter #1		▓	
	Letter #2		▓	
	Website			▓
Donors	Survey			
	Annual report			

CHAPTER 58.

PUT A BACKBONE IN CRISIS COMMUNICATION PLANS

Think about this. In today's world of instant, everywhere communication, serious, unexpected situations arise. Sometimes an organization finds itself in an array of media without boundaries. Such situations require prompt, principled, responsive behavior. Something needs to be added to crisis communication plans to give them the backbone to enable an organization to make quick responses. What a crisis communication plan needs is a code of conduct.

Trying to communicate in an unexpected, challenging situation without a code of conduct is what should be called crisis communication. The crisis is in trying to manage a tough situation without a strong set of guiding values and principles. What is needed is a rock solid established code of conduct to back up a good crisis communication plan. A code, at the ready and always in play, eliminates future panic over "What should we say? What shouldn't we say?" "We have to meet to decide!"

Relying on an established code of conduct doesn't mean changing lexicons from normal to crisis speak. It means having in place and practicing crisis-oriented core values and principles that are strong enough to weather any storm. Ideally, an organization should have a Crisis Code of Conduct and a Crisis Communication Plan.

Following is a draft code of conduct for you to use as a worksheet for developing a code appropriate for a profit or non-profit organization. The words in parentheses are placeholders, with three examples in each of five areas for values and principles. Each area could have any number, but keeping the code simple and brief makes it memorable and suited to pocket card and electronic device formats.

Draft Crisis Code of Conduct

(Organization Name) assesses difficult situations based on an established set of core values and principles. We consider all perspectives—organizational, individual, social and environmental. We align our thinking with the thinking of all of our stakeholder groups. Our core values clearly and simply express what we stand for and we rely on these values to guide our actions. When we align ourselves with our core values, it gives us energy and a sense of dedication to do what's right in resolving difficult situations. We know that critical decisions, backed by core values, are respected by all stakeholders as a display of an organization's true strength.

Our crisis core values are that we will be:

- (transparent in our actions);
- (accountable); and
- (empathetic).

Our crisis leadership principles are that our leader will

- (be visible and in charge immediately);
- (own up to responsibilities; and
- (lay out action steps).

Our crisis communication principles are that we will:

- (tell it all and tell it fast);
- (tell the whole truth up front); and
- (be accurate with the facts).

Our crisis media relations principles are that we will:

- (treat reporters as partners);
- (keep reporters informed); and
- (correct inaccurate reports).

Our crisis spokesperson principles are that we will:

- (treat everyone with respect);
- (be thoughtful and precise with words); and

- (listen as carefully as we speak and answer all questions to the best of our ability).

By making a code of conduct that backbone of a crisis communication plan, an organization can be at the ready to act responsibly in unexpected, reputation-challenging situations.

CHAPTER 59.

DISTINGUISH YOURSELF AS A NEWS MEDIA STRATEGIST

News Media Strategist

Following are tactics to enable you to distinguish yourself as a "news media strategist" in handling calls from reporters. In this chapter, you will learn how to decide in advance on the news source you want to be, or have to be, and how to maintain that position throughout a conversation with a journalist. For example, you might decide in advance of a press call that you want to be cooperative, but with nothing quotable to offer, or a source that has information that you would like to have published. You also will learn how to keep from being a news source you hadn't intended to be, by allowing yourself to be pulled off your position.

5   4   3   2   1   2   3   4   5

News Source Mental Marker

Above is a mental marker of news sources. Each source will be described so that when the news media call, you can imagine this display and mentally remind yourself what position, in a particular situation, you want to maintain as a news source. The News Source Mental Marker is meant to enable you to examine the relationship between yourself and a reporter and the process you are likely to engage as you address an issue. Prepare in advance and decide where you want or have to be on the marker.

Number 1 represents a news source that is not likely to offer quotable information. Reasons might be that this source is not expected to take a side on a particular issue, is bound by a restrictive press policy or is normally evasive in responding to questions. If you decide to be Number 1 on an issue, then think of the mental marker Number 1 and don't let yourself be persuaded to be pulled to a different position with a reporter saying, "Ah, come on. We've been working together for a long time. You can trust me with just a hint of what's going to happen." Another point to make is that the organization you represent might be at the center of an issue, yet no one is contacting you from the media, which might be because the media expects you to be a Number 1. If you must be a Number 1 on a particular issue, think of the many ways you can converse politely without blurting out, "No comment!" You should be able to talk in a comfortable manner with a reporter for five or 10 minutes or more without providing any quotable information or comment. As you are asked questions, visualize the Mental Marker and remind yourself repeatedly about what you must do to stay firmly on the mark.

5   4   3   2   1   2   3   4   5

News Source Mental Marker

There are two 2's, 3's, 4's and 5's to show that there are at least two sides to every issue. To a reporter, being objective means giving equal coverage to each side. If a reporter gets a comment from one side, the practice is to balance it with a comment from the other side.

Number 2 represents a news source of someone easily persuaded to make a comment. A reporter might attempt to draw a source from being a Number 1 to a Number 2—someone under a strict press policy, but could be persuaded to offer a comment when a reporter, for example, says, "I know you can't comment on rumors or speculation, but do you believe the public might see your organization as a potential target of the Justice Department?"

News Source Mental Marker

A Number 3 on this mental marker represents an ideal news source. A person in this position has credentials as a knowledgeable news source and is willing to express views publicly. Examples are doctors, lawyers, elected officials, press secretaries—individuals with professional backgrounds that give their statements credibility. Even their unsubstantiated opinions are considered quotable.

If your organization is at the center of a controversy and you haven't been called by the media, it could be because your organization is known for maintaining a low profile. So, if you want to comment, you must decide to be a Number 3 and take the initiative to call the press.

If the reporter can obtain quotable commentary on one side of an issue, common practice is to balance it with commentary from another side which, in a reporter's view, is being objective. Developing an article with comments from Number 3's is considered excellent reporting.

5 4 3 2 1 2 3 4 5

News Source Mental Marker

A Number 4 on the mental marker represents someone remotely associated with an issue, lightly informed, but willing to comment or render an opinion on it for publicity. A reporter, in an assertive manner, might try to use a Number 4 as a credible source—a Number 3. What should matter to you is to know that this is done and as a Number 3, you don't want to respond to a reporter's questions that seem to be from a Number 4—unfounded, speculative and self-serving. More on the dynamics later.

Number 5 news sources represent people with extreme views on an issue. It used to be that 5's were regarded by reporters to be somewhere on the lunatic fringe with opinions that weren't worthy of publicity. However, now that news programs are directed more as a form of entertainment, people on the fringe are becoming part of the show. Hopefully, reporters will continue to seek credible news sources.

5 4 3 2 1 2 3 4 5

News Source Mental Marker

Now let's look at some dynamics. Sometimes a reporter can verify information from credible sources on both sides of an issue. However, other times a reporter must rely on what he or she is told by sources on either side of an issue. This is important to know because if you are a Number 3 on one side of an issue you could be asked questions based not on facts, but on what the reporter has been told by sources on the other side, regardless of their veracity. A Number 2, for example, with weak credentials, limited factual and biased information, might want publicity and try to be a credible Number 3. A Number 4 with knowledge on the fringe of an issue might also try for publicity as a Number 3. A Number 5, with extreme, baseless views, and self-serving interests might also try for publicity as a Number 4. Motivation for these dynamics might come from a source or from a persuasive reporter or both. If you decide to engage in an issue, publicly, it is important to think about what kind of source the reporter is trying to get you to respond to. You certainly wouldn't want to engage on an issue with a Number 5. Remember, too, that engaging back and forth publicly with any source usually turns a story into a saga.

When you see yourself as a possible news source for an issue, decide before journalists call where you want to be on the news source mental marker.

Choose a position; expect pressure to change your position. When the wind starts to blow, think of the above marker and that will help you maintain your position.

If you are going to be a Number 1 and want to sleep at night, worry-free that you will not see your name in headlines in the morning, take a firm stand and never, without exception, offer anything off the record.

If you usually are a Number 1, but have a view that needs to be expressed, know that you most likely won't be contacted and that you will have to take the initiative to contact reporters as a Number 3.

If you think you want to challenge a reporter for objectivity, think again about what objectivity means to a reporter in covering an issue—generally an equal number of comments from each side of the issue. Make sure your challenge has a clear basis, such as accuracy.

CHAPTER 60.

AFRAID TO CRITIQUE ADVERTISING PROPOSALS? IF SO, WHY?

As a public relations professional, why might you be afraid to speak up and critique advertising proposals? Could it be that you believe that advertising is someone else's area of expertise? Could it be that you feel that you don't have a degree in advertising to be able to offer intelligent criticisms or understand advertising jargon, terms or practices to be able to make good comments? If you find yourself indulging in excuses such as these, it's probably time to rethink your position. The following headline and image about Carl's Jr.'s use of Paris Hilton in one of the company's commercials will give us an actual example to discuss this in more detail.

Paris Hilton Returns in a New Carl's Jr. Commercial

When you first saw Paris Hilton featured in a TV commercial for Carl's Jr., did it raise questions in your mind like, "I wonder who signed off on this idea?" "Does this represent the CEO's thinking?" "Does this appeal to customers and families?" "Does this represent the thinking of the board of directors?" "What are expectations of this ad by investors and the financial community?" If you had had an opportunity, as a PR professional, to comment on a proposal featuring Paris Hilton as shown above in an ad for Carl's Jr., would you have questioned the proposal or would you have said, "Advertising is beyond my area of expertise?"

If you had something to say about the proposed commercial, but passed on the opportunity, why would you do that?

Here's one way to look at this. As a professional communicator you have many communication "tools" at your disposal. Advertising is one of them. It's true that advertising is cloaked in its own lingo, just like lawyers speak in legalese, financial experts dance around stilted terms and engineers geek it up a bit. But when you get right down to it, a goal is a goal, an objective is an objective and a strategy is a strategy. What presents a challenge is that within and among professions, definitions of these terms are anything but universally clear. Nevertheless, they should not keep you from critiquing advertising with basic communication terms as you understand them in public relations.

The advertising function might reside in a public relations or advertising department. Advertising, wherever it is created, in-house or by an outside agency, is aimed an influencing human behavior, like public relations, and a proposal or plan is organized under the same elements of goals, objectives, strategies, tactics, timelines, measurements and evaluations. An objective, for example, should tell what must be done to achieve a public relations or advertising goal. A strategy should tell how an objective is to be achieved. Activities should provide the steps to be carried out in a strategy. These basic terms should be so clear, for example, that you should be able to ask to have the objective of a print ad written in one sentence on the back of a comp (comprehensive layout) and be able to flip the comp over to the ad side and in a second or two say, "Yes, this ad will achieve our objective." If not, back it goes to the creative department. As a trained communicator, you have all the background necessary to express a professional critique of advertising proposals and you should do it with confidence.

CHAPTER 61.

AVOID OUTRAGE—KNOW THE DIFFERENCE BETWEEN RISK AND CRISIS COMMUNICATION

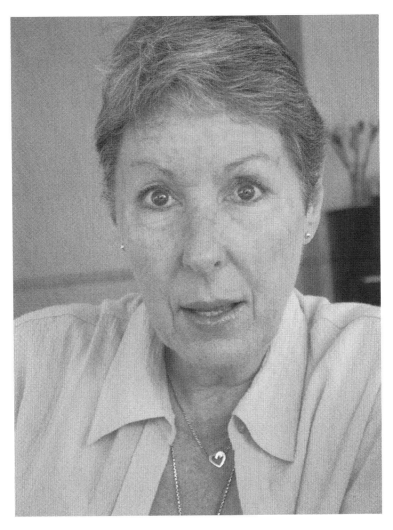

Communicators, especially entry-professionals, must know the difference between risk communication and crisis communication. There is a bank of knowledge on these two subjects, but the intent of this article is to point out the fundamental difference and provide advice to keep you from getting into a situation and unwittingly incite public outrage.

So, what's the difference? Risk communication deals with things that *might* go wrong. Crisis communication deals with things that have gone wrong.

Risk communication responds to any event that could cause public concern and could focus media attention on an organization. Steps must be taken to inform people about hazards to their environment, safety or health, manage potential problems in a manner that promotes goodwill, disseminate information, encourage prudent action and reduce panic.

Risk communication skills and techniques are used to handle both risk and crisis situations. With risk communication, communicators lay the groundwork for trust between the community and the organization dealing with the risks involved. Poor risk communication could cause a crisis communication episode to develop.

Here are examples of each, courtesy of the University of Florida:

Risk Communication

You own a food processing facility. A food product a competitor sells has been found to have salmonella. The competing company issues a food recall. Your product is free of salmonella; nevertheless, you realize that the concern about salmonella connected to this product generally will inevitably affect your company, so you go into "risk communication" mode. You initiate a toll-free telephone hotline, informational websites, and distribution of information through various media to inform consumers that your product is safe. You are being proactive and are listening to and responding to the public. Because you act quickly to bring the public in as a partner, concern about your product is alleviated. Sales decrease in the immediate aftermath and you suffer some economic loss, but because you have responded in a way that enhances the public's trust, you are seen as a responsible company and recover quickly.

Crisis Communication

Your food processing company unknowingly shipped out salmonella-tainted food. Within a short time, people around the country are getting sick, and the cause has been traced to your company. You are in "crisis communication" mode. In this scenario, you must respond quickly to the media and the public's food safety concerns. If you respond in a way that addresses their concerns, you can maintain credibility and trust.

Four factors critical in risk communication

There are four areas, in particular, to pay special attention in communicating risk. Overlooking or mishandling even one is likely to result in public outrage.

In public gatherings and meetings, it is important to treat every person's question, no matter how relevant or how trivial one might seem, with genuine interest and respect. Know that it is most important to address a person's emotion first and then the question (e.g. "I can see how deeply stressed you are over this situation.") If a question, which has already been asked, is asked again, treat it as though it is being asked for the first time. Try to satisfy or promise to satisfy the source with as much information as requested. Keep in mind that there could be related issues that might be more important to people than the risk itself. In question and answer sessions, stay as long as necessary to answer the last question. Saying, "That's all we have time for," is unacceptable to persons at risk.

It is thought by some that putting a person with impeccable credentials before an anxious audience will reduce stress and open a door to constructive dialogue. This is seldom true. In tense environments, people are more inclined to listen to and follow a "friend" of the community who is known and trusted for openness, honesty, integrity and empathy.

Such a leader can bring others in with appropriate credentials to help work on an issue. Know that in risk and crisis situations, people want to hear not from spokespersons, but directly from the person in charge (e.g. incident commander, police chief, local Red Cross director, fire chief, hospital director, etc.)

The head of an organization must be able to speak about risk from a foundation of evidence that supports every claim to be made about health and safety standards, performance records and achievements of an organization. People can easily detect dishonest representation of the facts. Make doubly sure the leader can honestly and accurately speak from evidence that substantiates all claims of good conduct.

People in risk situations feel more comfortable about accepting a degree of risk when they have or are given some control over a situation. The control could be a citizens' advisory board, oversight by an appropriate authority, periodic reviews and public reports, well-designed liaison with government services.

Overlooking or mishandling even one of the four factors above is likely to result in public outrage.

TWO EXCELLENT SOURCES FOR FURTHER RESEARCH

Peter M. Sandman is one of the preeminent risk communication speakers and consultants in the United States today. (www.psandman.com)

Document WC093, July 2010/reviewed November 2016, one of a series of the Agricultural Education and Communication Department, University of Florida, Institute of Food and Agriculture Sciences (http://edis.ifas.ufl.edu).

CHAPTER 62.

WHY FACTS DON'T CHANGE OUR MINDS

James Clear wrote an article that is of particular interest in today's highly charged political climate. Clear begins his article, "Why Facts Don't Change Our Minds," asking these questions:

What's going on here? Why don't facts change our minds?

And why would someone continue to believe a false or inaccurate idea anyway? How do such behaviors serve us?

To promote discussion and analysis, here are excerpts from his responses to these timely questions:

· We don't always believe things because they are correct. Sometimes we believe things because they make us look good to the people we care about.

· When we have to choose between the two [factually false and socially accurate] people often select friends and family over facts.

· Convincing someone to change their mind is really the process of convincing them to change their tribe. If they abandon their beliefs, they run the risk of losing social ties. You can't expect someone to change their mind if you take away their community too.

· The way to change people's minds is to become friends with them, to integrate them into your tribe, to bring them into your circle.

· ...books are often a better vehicle for transforming beliefs than conversations or debates... When confronted with an uncomfortable set of facts, the tendency is often to double down on their current position rather than publicly admit to being wrong. Books resolve this tension. With a book, the conversation takes place inside someone's head and without the risk of being judged by others. It's easier to be open-minded when you aren't feeling defensive.

·   There is another reason bad ideas continue to live on, which is that people continue to talk about them. Silence is death for any idea. An idea that is never spoken or written down dies with the person who conceived it… They can only be believed when they are repeated… Before you can criticize an idea, you have to reference that idea. You end up repeating the ideas you are hoping people will forget—but, of course, people can't forget them because you keep talking about them. The more you repeat a bad idea, the more likely people are to believe it. Let's call this phenomenon Clear's Law of Recurrence…

·   …you want to criticize bad ideas because you think the world would be better off if fewer people believed them… If the goal is to actually change minds, then I don't believe criticizing the other side is the best approach. Most people argue to win, not to learn.

Take this link to read the full article by James Clear:

https://jamesclear.com/why-facts-dont-change-minds

CHAPTER 63.

NUGGETS OF WISDOM

tomhagley@gmail.com

Some of what Tom Hagley Sr. has learned over four decades as a public relations practitioner and educator could be of value in helping you learn from the School of Experience, rather than from the School of Hard Knocks. From these lessons learned one can derive advice, comfort, knowledge, guidance, wisdom, tips, a nudge here and there, reassurance, insight, support and more.

1. To succeed in an organization, you must be seen, heard and well sponsored—championed.

2. Sometimes all you need to feel better about work is a good burger.

3. Do what your client or employer wants. Do it well

and deliver on time. Far exceeding expectations and beating deadlines to impress isn't necessary and only keeps you from balancing your professional with your personal life.

4. If you want to be seen as a consultant, rather than a technician, don't carry a pencil behind the ear, a clipboard in hand and a camera around your neck.

5. Only birds can wing it. Use every minute available to prepare in advance for an opportunity to comment or express an opinion.

6. Public relations is the practice of influencing behavior through strategic communication.

7. Trusting your career to someone else, for example, believing that someone has a career path for you in the top desk drawer, is like believing in Santa Claus. Chart your own course.

8. The quick acquisition of knowledge from today's world of readily available resources, is a powerful tool.

9. Clients pay consultants top dollar and expect 100 percent of their presence; use or even sight of a consultant's cell phone is considered by some clients as rude, intrusive, cavalier—anything but respectful. Walking away and saying, "I've got to take this," says to a client, "There's something more important than you."

10. In PR, entry professionals can progress faster in their careers than others when they work where there are PR professionals to mentor and cham-

pion their development.

11. Write the song and let the client take the bow.

12. Job seekers should know that for an employer, hiring an employee has risks: it's a training investment with an unknown return; it's a reflection on an employer's ability to judge qualified job candidates; it's a bet on bringing in more business. You can reduce the risk by expressing your interest in the job, your confidence in being able to do the work, and your desire to contribute to the success of the organization.

13. Attention to detail is what makes an event memorable.

14. Influencing on the merits is always the way to win.

15. When taking an opposing stand, always attack the issue and not its sponsor. You might need the sponsor on your side for some other issue.

16. If it's not in the public interest, don't do it.

17. Sometimes your ego can hold you accountable beyond reason.

18. Learn to take risks.

19. Corporate career plans can be a figment of your imagination, unless you take charge of your own future.

20. Changing jobs has value, but so does experience in and knowledge of a single industry.

21. There's only one way to make a good impres-

sion–honestly.

22. High visibility errors are painful but not life-threatening.

23. See obstacles as challenges to work around to reach your goal.

24. Job transfers can provide career progress, but roots in a community are valuable too.

25. Sometimes what you have is much better than what you think you have.

26. Something you did or failed to do might be forgiven, but is never forgotten.

27. In a job interview, if you like the work, the people and the place, say so: "I would love to work here!"

28. To win trust, an organization must be transparent, accountable and authentic.

29. Look for a pearl in every oyster and savor the search.

30. When you finally think it's perfect, it's time to check it again.

31. To have standards, a profession must have a definable purpose.

32. Others harbor an ignorant view until you teach them what you do.

33. Promise only what you know you can deliver.

34. Older isn't necessarily wiser; trust your own judgement.

35. Your ideas are good. Offer them free of qualifica-

tions and apologies for their possible value.

36. Search for good interpersonal chemistry; the job will follow.

37. Life is imperfect, often better than it seems; don't let impatience rob you of what you have.

38. You have a mind to decide what you want to be to others. Think what you want to be to others before you act or speak. Try to maintain a predictable and consistent character.

FOR PR FACULTY THE PLAYBOOK CAN BE LIKE A TEACHING ASSISTANT

Public Relations Faculty!

While the Playbook is written to enable students to excel in class and at work, for you it can be like getting a teaching assistant. Look at the book from your perspective as an instructor and think about how the chapters can save you time preparing and conducting class activities and discussions, developing syllabi, teaching AP style, having students give you what you need to easily and quickly write good recommendation letters. Use it to show students how to improve their public relations writing, take an interest the latest concepts like on-line community engagement and on-line networks with influencers. Consider how you can use chapters to show students how to teach themselves to make the most of class time, how to get along, develop plans, organize and present in teams, create their own career success strategies. Use the Playbook to give students an unvarnished look at the profession. The Playbook truly is like getting a teaching assistant.

Best wishes, Tom

tomhagley@gmail.com

NEW 3RD EDITION WRITING WINNING PROPOSALS: PUBLIC RELATIONS CASES

Writing Winning Proposals: Public Relations Cases,

new 3rd edition by Rebecca A. Gilliland and Thomas R. Hagley, teaches students, as well as practitioners, how to conceptualize and write public relations plans and proposals from the perspective of the plan reviewer — typically non-public relations practitioners. The process illustrated within the book is designed to win approval from the plan reviewers and to foster a path for award-winning plan writing. The book thoroughly describes components of the plan, and then provides many actual cases to further demonstrate the strategy and thought process behind plan construction.

The cases have multiple suggested writing assignments, role plays, and case problems. These help students and practitioners explore progression of plan construction in various avenues where public relations may be required and practiced. Cases highlighting community relations and engagement, media relations, employee relations and empowerment, government relations, crisis management and prevention, risk communication, corporate communication, social media implementation, arts and entertainment, corporate communication, social responsibility, promotional endeavors, and event planning are all included. Writing Winning Proposals is ideal for introductory public relations courses, as well as courses in public relations writing, plans, and campaigns. It can also be used as an academic text supplement, a campaigns workbook, or for strategic planning.

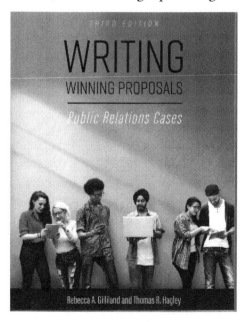

Rebecca A. Gilliland is a distinguished professor of service learning and an associate professor of communication at the University of Indianapolis. A Fulbright Scholar and a Plank Fellow, Professor Gilliland has traveled the United States and around the world in an effort to stay current in the public relations industry while studying her areas of interest. She advises a nationally award-winning student run public relations firm and has taught numerous public relations classes. She has worked abroad and domestically, in sports promotions, corporate public relations, and in the non-profit sector. She is accredited in public relations and earned a doctorate in education with cognates in both public relations and communication studies.

Thomas R. Hagley is a senior instructor of public relations retired from the University of Oregon's School of Journalism and Communication. The recipient of the school's Jonathan Marshall Award for innovative teaching has taught more than 50 classes in public relations principles, advanced writing, strategic planning, and campaigns to a total enrollment of more than 1,000 students. His work as an educator was preceded by 30 years of professional experience as an executive with Alumax, Inc., Hill and Knowlton, Inc., his own consulting business, Alcoa, as publications chief for Newport News Shipbuilding and Dry Dock Co., and general assignment/investigative reporter for The Cleveland Plain Dealer.

View digital copies of their book:

Cognella Academic Publishing

Amazon Prime

https://titles.cognella.com/writing-winning-proposals-9781516516360.html

View book at Amazon

*View book at Cognella
Academic Publishing*

Made in the USA
Middletown, DE
10 January 2020

82892478R00210